THE CURE-ALL FOR THE

Relationship
PANDEMIC

THE RIGHT RELATIONSHIP MEANS EVERYTHING!

DR. LLOYD SLOWE

The Cure-All for the Relationship Pandemic
Copyright © 2024 by Dr. Lloyd Slowe

All rights reserved. No part of this publication may be reproduced, distributed, or transmitted in any form or by any means, including photocopying, recording, or other electronic or mechanical methods, without the prior written permission of the author, except in the case of brief quotations embodied in critical reviews and certain other non-commercial uses permitted by copyright law.

Library of Congress Control Number: 2024918974

ISBN
978-1-964488-26-4 (Paperback)
978-1-964488-27-1 (eBook)
978-1-964488-25-7 (Hardcover)

TABLE OF CONTENTS

Preface vii

1. Why Is Preparation for a Relationship Necessary? 1
2. Question Yourself 16
3. Am I Really Ready for a Relationship? 27
4. Why Do I Think That I Am Ready? 39
5. What Do I Want from a Relationship? 50
6. What Do I Have to Offer in a Relationship? 64
7. Evaluating Your Relationship through the SWOT Analysis 78
8. Mental Readiness: Am I Really Mentally Ready? 94
9. Am I Physically Ready for a Relationship? 103
10. Am I Financially Ready for a Relationship? 110
11. Am I Morally Ready for a Relationship? 124
12. Am I Emotionally Ready for a Relationship? 132
13. Dignity Preservation in a Relationship 143
14. What Is the Path to Preserving Dignity in Relationships? 161
15. Understanding a Relationship's Protocol 178

Conclusion 195

PREFACE

One of the greatest decisions in life is marriage. It is undeniably popular and has been for centuries. Because of the complexities of most cultures, particularly in the western hemisphere, preparation for marriage is not a path to be taken lightly.

This book is intended to mirror those internal and external images that directly and indirectly reflect the process, challenges, and other approaches to marriage that one must be willing to take on, prior to making this lifetime commitment.

It is hoped that this book will help you to appreciate how preparation can expose vulnerabilities and sensitivities that were deeply buried. Ultimately, it is to help you discover your greatest virtue and if indeed that includes marriage, how to be your best at it.

You will be guided through the different ways in which you can identify a suitable partner for a sustainable, long-term, and resilient relationship that, having survived the many unavoidable challenges, may culminate in marriage and saying, "I do."

Let's start this journey together.

1. WHY IS PREPARATION FOR A RELATIONSHIP NECESSARY?

Life is filled with pitfalls. In every step of our journey, there is some form of challenge. One of the greatest mistakes many make is seeking relationship is not to consider or adequately prepare themselves in all ways before venturing into the lifetime commitment that is marriage.

Preparation has to do with the action or process of making ready for use or consideration, considering the complexities of our lives. Without preparation, success is unlikely. Consider preparation the cornerstone of a man's destiny. If you hate preparation, then you do not love success.

As an example, let's revisit going to school. Prior to moving on to the next class, one of the criteria is a test to show what you have learned. Not preparing for that test means you will be less confident and more nervous. This lack of preparedness can manifest in many ways, such as you not successfully completing the course or having to identify some consistently weak areas that need work. You may even be intimidated by not knowing some of the answers or feel guilty for not knowing since you had time to prepare. If you fail your exams, you will have to repeat a year instead of going to the next, more advanced grade with your friends.

A marriage is similar. It doesn't signify the end of a relationship but the beginning of a new chapter for which you must prepare adequately and which you must consistently work to keep in its space.

God wants us to achieve success, which is another reason to prepare before taking that sacred vow before God and man by saying, "I do." It is equally important for both parties to understand and appreciate the importance of their roles in preparation for such life-changing decisions. Ephesians 5:23 (NKJV) tells us, "For the husband is the head of the wife, as also Christ is the head of the Church, and He is the Savior of the body." In this context, "head" refers to having leadership or authority. That is the role of the man. God wants man to be the prophet, priest, and king of his household since he will now become responsible for his wife and family. With leadership comes responsibilities, and the man being the head means that he is a team player as opposed to him being superior to his wife and just existing to be Lord over her.

In the same way, God is the head of the church. The church was founded by God and is defended by Him. He will defend the church at all costs. There is no contrast between God and man in the verse but a degree of similarity that speaks specifically to authority and responsibility. Once you have a certain level of authority, as is given by God to men, that authority cannot be casually handled. Preparing yourself for whatever comes is key.

Even though marriage is popular, it remains an unknown territory. for first-timers. It is important to prepare for the best and most ideal outcomes. You must also prepare for the intensely challenging moments so that your relationship has a chance of recovery and builds its resilience. The adage "Failing to prepare is preparing to fail" could not be more appropriate. When someone says, "Give me six hours to chop down a tree," in their mind, they dedicate an hour to sharpening their ax. That is preparation. Otherwise, they would be using a dull ax, which then makes chopping down the tree take twice as long.

The most fundamental reason for marital demise is lack of preparation. It cannot be emphasized enough, and both the man and the woman must equally prepare.

Preparing to say, "I do," is almost like being a soldier standing ready and poised for the battle he committed to fight—much like the soldier described in Ephesians 6:11 (NKJV): He is commanded by the Commander to put on the whole armor of God. He girded his waist with Truth, put on the breastplate of Righteousness, shod his feet with the preparation of the Gospel, taking the shield of Faith, the helmet of Salvation and the sword of the Spirit, which is the Word of God, and most importantly prayer and supplication. This is the way he dresses in spirit and manifests in the flesh.

In my sixteen years of pastoral ministry, I have witnessed many relationships meeting their untimely demise in divorce because of insufficient preparation. Because of that firsthand witness account, I have set a precedent for married couples as well as the betrothed ones. Prior to their making a commitment, it became a requirement for at least three sessions of professional or pastoral counseling. These sessions pave the way for the sustainability of the relationship. It is a common occurrence where men believe they have all areas covered when they approach the commitment only to realize midway through that it is not so. It is prudent to note that there should be no shame in admitting that you are not ready, as a man or woman, for a commitment, and it would be best to admit that as early as possible in the relationship. It would serve you both better to invest the time to make yourselves ready for that next step rather than rush the "I do" and spend twice as much time trying to make up for mistakes or lessons learned that could have been avoided.

Thanks be to God the first couple who sat with me at the beginning of their journey in marriage are still happily married. I feel privileged to have been included in their journey and to witness their marriage's sustenance. Those of us who put in the work to prepare and end up lasting longer know there is no magic word or luck involved in making a relationship last our lifetimes. Exchanging vows is serious not only before man but also before God, and the stakes involved if this marriage does not last are thus high. This means the concept of marriage shouldn't be thrown around but instead regarded with the sovereignty on which it was created.

Imagine the time spent as well as the scars, pain, and emotional havoc that come from a divorce, in most cases. And usually, the state of the relationship until its ultimate demise is bitter, for both parties. May I insert that divorce is worst that death. Because when someone dies, that chapter of life is closed forever. But every time exes who are divorced sees or thinks about the past their toxic emotions resurrected again. That is heartbreaking, even more so when children are involved. Children who are products of such ill-fated marriages suffer years after the breakup because of the trauma they carry, sometimes into adulthood. I ask, "Who wins?" It is painfully clear that no one does.

And it hurts no one to adequately prepare.

A more recent account of my sessions on relationships and marriages includes a young man who was pouring out his heart to me as he explained the pains he was going through in his divorce, even admitting violence was involved. After we reasoned it out, I was able to identify a few red flags. That was because they were left unattended. Regrettably, divorce was inevitable.

The first mistake some men make is confusing infatuation for love and basing important decisions on that confused notion. This is when there is an unprepared disposition to the entire approach of the relationship, and men rely heavily on infatuation to guide their plans. Infatuation, though intense, is short-lived and while it may last for months, considering it against the year spent in a bitter marriage, it is indeed a short period of time.

Other observations from this young man that we could learn from include looking out for red flags, such as lack of responsibility, immaturity, infidelity, lack of compassion, and lack of a love language.

All these could have been highlighted had this relationship gone through the stages of preparation, but alas, he discovered them at the end. Of course, addressing such issues is a part of the preparation, as failing to do so means they will come out in a marriage, which will then nosedive. Once it does, that means years of pain and simply years that cannot be regained. One vital tool of the enemy, in the context of divorced couples, is an acute episode of depression; tragically, sometimes, it leads to suicide. There are enough cases to support a correlation between the two, and it is not surprising.

Consider also that marriage is an institution of God, yet our church population has increasingly high rates of divorce because of lack of preparation. Isn't it something that the teachings of marriage are from God, yet His own followers get divorced often? That certainly doesn't breed confidence among the unmarried members and outsiders looking in—the very people these churches are trying to reach. Again, it is okay to say that you don't feel ready. While you are preparing, your confidence may grow, or it may wane, but it is better to do so before the finality that is usually associated with saying, "I do." Agreed?

It is this sense of failure that propels me to encourage precedence of raising children so they are groomed into responsible human beings and better equipped with handling commitments; their adult selves will be grateful for it. It is crucial to have a sense of responsibility from as early as possible to blossom into a responsible adult. It is harder for adults learn the intricacies of responsibilities when they are already set in their ways. Grooming a responsible child can be subtle and rewarding for the child. Chores have always been rewarding, fulfilling, and appropriate teachers of responsibilities.

It is not lost on me that parents themselves either need to be taught responsibility or are aware of but choose to ignore their responsibilities as adults and see no harm in having children and rearing them in this toxic manner.

The time is now for a shift to happen regarding how the men and women of tomorrow are groomed. Families are the very fabric of our society, and while we don't groom children for marriage from too early, they can certainly be prepared by teaching them to be responsible, humble, and patient, which makes them better, more well-rounded adults. As adults, we must agree on this, and this agreement can be reflected in our educational manuals and, of course, at church. Challenges in the home have a ripple effect as individuals maneuver through life and affect the many subjects they touch their hands to. This interconnectedness is how I can say with certainty that deficiencies in the home will most certainly touch different aspects of society for as long as the deficiency lasts.

Permit me to also declare that education, in all it stands for, plays a crucial role in social reform. Marriage is a social institution, as it may soon become a family unit and so the cycle continues. So, with that logic, in order to mitigate high divorce rates, we need to agree on education as early as possible on all the tenets that would then lead to more sustainable marriages.

Another essential item for your tool kit is a mentor. A mentor is someone you wish to emulate. The younger generations gravitate to the counsel of their peers, who lack the added benefit of someone with more experience on the subject. Titus 2:2–5 (NKJV) admonishes the older men to "be sober, reverent, temperate, sound in faith, in love, in patience, and to exhort the young men to be sober-minded in all things unto a pattern of good works." He also admonishes the elder women to be reverent in their behaviors, not slanderous, and not given to too much wine and to teach good things and young women to love their husbands and their children, to be discreet, chaste, homemakers, good, and obedient to their husbands so that the word of God be not blasphemed. A happier and healthier society, a place where marriages thrived and the number of divorces decreased, would be more achievable if we all could take a line from Titus.

Now there is no journey like the one walked. I can tout the benefits of preparation all day, but having walked that path is what renews my confidence in the process. Before saying "I do" to my wife, my fundamental method of preparation was through fasting and prayer, asking God to lead me to the woman of my dreams. Sure enough, it was not much longer after that I saw who my wife was to be through a dream, and the rest is history, as we continue this immense journey. I am celebrating thirty-three years of marriage so far, and there have been no regrets. We get better at marriage as we grow older and embrace learning together. Fasting and praying have been my partners for preparedness, as I have learned more through that process than without it. I prayed to the one true and living God, the author of the institution of marriage, according to Matthew 19:5 (NKJV) "For this reason, a man shall leave his father and mother and join unto his wife and the two shall become one flesh."

To paint you a vivid picture: imagine two negative partners joining together versus two positive ones. You can find out what your partner is if you are willing to discern before rushing to "I do." Comprehensive preparation will eliminate much stress, anger, bitterness, and heartache if you just put in the work.

Another aspect of preparation is self-identity. For both men and women, you need to know who you are as an individual person before you can find out what type of partner you would make and what type of partner you would want. You have to discover your likes and dislikes, your personality, your temperament. Would you classify your moods as constantly changing, or are you pretty much the same most of the time? What do you enjoy doing for fun, and what type of work would you love to do? All these questions need answers, and the best person to find them is you—with the help of others, of course. But primarily, you must at least have a clue. You get better results by admitting your strengths and weaknesses. Then you know what you need to do to become a better version of yourself. If you are like me, you do a self-assessment and make notes of what you wish to improve and adjust. Sometimes, when you have no sense of direction or solution, you do as I do and approach the problem with prayer and fasting.

It never hurts to examine your thoughts, even those you wouldn't readily admit to having, either to yourself or out loud, and consider their implications on the type of partner you would be and the consequences for the relationship. Consider entering a relationship like a physical examination for the military, where you must pass in order to apply or get that promotion The army requires it because they would like to know the status of your health, to determine if you are fit to serve physically. In the same way, you must examine yourself to ensure that you know exactly what you are capable of and what needs fixing. That is, you are preparing to become a better version of yourself, to become a better partner.

It is counterproductive to enter a relationship knowing full well you both have baggage that is unaddressed or that you are unwilling to address. How else do you expect your marriage to have a chance? How can you wonder why the relationship is so tumultuous from the beginning when you have no conscious thought of who you are and how that would work for or against the relationship you and your partner want to have? The answers are usually simple and right before your eyes. Additionally, entering a relationship with clear expectations communicated between you and your partner, coupled with a firm understanding of your limits and their implications, helps to set the tone for less wondering and more active work being done on the matters that you can work on. It is like how your doctor would ask for the history of diagnoses in your family before making a diagnosis in direct relation to your medical complaint. Similar principles suit approaching a marriage.

I have another analogy: athletes spend weeks and months in training before competitions, so they can bring their best to their game, even if they don't or won't win. The principle is similar in approaching marriages. It would be very egotistic, if not borderline delusional, to be competing with a renowned world or Olympic champion without preparation and yet expecting to win. If sportsmen and sportswomen can appreciate the need to train, how much more important is preparation in approaching a lifetime commitment where you vow to love another person for the rest of your life? Or even closer to home, can you win a court case without preparing your complaint or defense?

Often in relationships, even leading up to marriage, we blindly accept promises without realizing the disservice it does to us. It's like pleading a case before a judge, wherein you truthfully and tactfully loaned your best friend $5,000 and verbally agreed to repay within X amount of time. When X time had passed and there was no repayment, your best friend could easily say that was never the arrangement. You know in your heart it was, but you have no proof, and seeing that, you rely on the judge to settle the matter. Without proof, the judge has no choice but to rule as evidence or lack thereof dictates.

Everyone was born with flaws, all mired with imperfections, but you should always strive to be a better version of yourself every opportunity you get. I implore you. And even if the situation does not present an opportunity, invent one. When planning to begin a relationship, improvements, and adjustments to yourself should be your priority. Would you want to live with the version of yourself that remains stagnant, with no exploration or self-improvement? If you are given to drinking, would you want to live with yourself? How then can you expect your partner to want to live with you? God expects us to improve, as in Philippians 4:13 (NKJV): "I can do all things through Christ who strengthens me." Just as you need Christ for your journey to self-improvement, you also need friends who are on the same path as you, to support you and facilitate your impending growth as you look toward maturity and growth. A friend indeed would be one who can anticipate and endure the stress and sometimes lack of progress, while you toil toward a better you, an improved version you can be proud of. This form of emotional support is represented through love, acceptance, encouragement, and reassurance. It promotes and strengthens your capability for different types of relationships and exposes you to stability. It also makes you appreciate that stability when you get it.

Choose friends who are mature and like-minded, preferably those with positive demonstrations of meeting the requirements within the relationship dynamic, specifically long-term relationships. Having the ability to understand and share emotions with another is not always an innate talent; it often must be learned and honed, so surround yourselves with friends who can appreciate wanting to learn and facilitate that growth process. A person who has walked the path you are walking or wants to walk it and discover it with you is someone you need in your corner. Keep him or her there.

Historically, women have been more giving, thus assuming the role of providing emotional support. I caution that even though you may find friends who are willing to offer emotional support, it will only satisfy some of your emotional needs. You will know that you are ready for the next level of intimacy once you can identify the areas of emotional support provided by friends and those that remain lacking. Your friend will not be able to do everything for you. Be willing to accept that fact. If, despite the emotional support, you somehow still feel inadequate within yourself or are still plagued with doubt, then the process needs more work.

Women may have an advantage in that they easily empathize and soothe in ways that make it seem effortless. In contrast, the men of today may not be as open to admitting problems of any nature or seeking advice in any form. It is just not the type of discussion that a man would initiate with specific focus on their problems. Admitting that he needs help does not come as naturally to a man. Even admitting doubt does not come easily to him. It is debatable that men were intentionally made different from women.

Some ways you can alleviate or overcome doubt are to believe in something within yourself and pick something that makes you feel as though you are winning when you accomplish it. Perseverance and tenacity must be your staples during this time; your ability will be honed by being able to get up after falling in your attempt and getting up with lessons learned. Have you ever heard the saying "A quitter never wins, and the winner never quits"? It has merit.

Another way to affirm yourself and your potential is, you guessed it, helping someone. Being able to identify ways in which you can help someone else through his or her distress or challenges helps you, because it shows you what you are capable of. Imagine if it was you.

Imagine what you could do with yourself. Providing emotional support to someone else is vital in a relationship, once it is balanced.

For it to be balanced, you must both know what you are looking for and what you are prepared to give. Otherwise, it is frustrating—and even more so if you are hesitant in communicating your wants and expectations but also what you offer. Unless you can read minds, that is. It would be safer to assume that your would-be long-term partner also cannot read minds; hence you need to communicate and do so as clearly as possible. Men are much more direct with communicating their wants, bordering on aggressive on occasions. Women tend to be less direct and more repressed in expressing their wants and needs, sometimes resulting in a pattern of emotional neglect for failure to communicate.

This potential for neglect is exacerbated when, not only does the partner not communicate, but the partner doesn't have a clear grasp of what he or she wants from the relationship, a contributing factor to being unable to communicate it clearly. Again, the chances of human beings reading minds are still very low. In the meantime, such a relationship as described here, already filled with neglect, will then translate to sadness, lack of fulfillment, and repressed frustration and anger, if the cycle is continuously fed, culminating in its own demise. Preparation at the beginning, however, could have informed both parties if they were moving in the same or opposite directions and what the preferred changes would have been like along the way.

If you have an inkling that you may not fully know what you are looking for, then it never hurts to start with the basics. Of course, there is no cure-all from one method, as we all have multiple layers, but start with the simple preferences; it stimulates your mind to think beyond the simple. This is good, as it is a better and stronger start than not knowing. Basic things to consider include if you prefer or are more compatible with a tall or short partner, a more introverted or extroverted partner, and if you are open to dating people from other cultures, or if you prefer those with whom you share a similar cultural experience. Along that line. Additional examples would be do you know anything about the background of the person you are contemplating a lifetime commitment to? Does he or she seem to handle stress in stride or get frustrated right off the bat? Are you open to a partner pursuing more traditional forms of employment or career lifestyles, or are you open to a less traditional form of employment? How hard would it be for you to support such a partner? And what exactly would be your grounds for anxiety if any?

All these are simple questions from the get-go, and if you think that sounds like too much work, how else would you be prepared for the more complex sides that will exist and manifest themselves in your relationship?

Having a detailed list of these simple things would help you navigate as you consider whether the person you are currently dating could be a long-term partner or if you want to go out into the dating world looking for a long-term partner. A list functions as a base, as your thoughts and emotions are constantly changing. This list serves as a reference point. Whenever you feel directionless or off course, you can simply go back to this base. Seeing your desires and expectations on paper reinforces and reaffirms that this is what you are or are willing to build with, and once you see your desires reflected on paper, then you have little need to test the waters, especially with someone you never would imagine yourself with. A bonus with your list is that you can always reprioritize as you see fit.

You may seem very interested in entering this preparation phase, but I urge you, if you intend to sugarcoat your desires on paper, then that is a counterproductive move from the get-go. Trying to sugarcoat what you are willing to bring to the relationship is also counterproductive to your would-be partner, who may be more invested and detailed in his or her expectations. Your would-be partner would also, if he or she is trying to prepare for a long-term relationship, take note and pay attention to details he or she deems important from the initial stages, and you must be cognizant of that fact.

Take me, for example. When I met my to-be wife almost thirty-three years ago, I was impressed by what I saw, coupled with my revelation that she was to be my wife. I still recall it vividly, like it was yesterday: her speech, her deportment, and more so, how she regarded me. She was very collected and seemed purposeful, and her confidence was evident. I was immediately intrigued. It is important to emphasize the need to always be the best version of yourself always but also to always be a correct version of yourself, not a facade. Imagine God showing me my wife years ago, and we met and felt a connection, yet for months, I would see a personality emerge that was 180 degrees

It would be understandable that I would have questions and concerns and would seek to address them before we could move on to say, "I do." Thankfully that didn't happen, and my wife and I went on to say, "I do."

Conversely, even if I were to see all the signs put before me and everything I wanted was consistently presented before me, if I had doubts of my own worth, of deserving this woman of my dreams, then that could have been powerful enough to see me missing out on a love of a lifetime. Remember to be kind to yourself, and when assessing your own worth, do so from within. Assess not only your looks, your money, and your power but who you are as a human and the type of soul you would want to connect with. This requires good judgment and the ability to grasp what is most important at the end of the day. It is better to ask these self-exploratory questions before committing long term, as your partner may ask, and it would be fairer to him or her if you had an answer or an idea of the answer.

It would alleviate more anxiety if you were able to be honest with whom you have come to identify as a human being. Sooner or later, your partner may either draw his or her own conclusions or see the progress you are trying to make considering how you were when you had just met. Be honest, always. This honesty, I implore you, must always start with yourself. Only when you have his sense of honesty can you be prepared to give complete honesty to your partner; you both deserve it.

This brings me to another staple in the preparation phase: communication. I purposefully encouraged introspection before anything else, because of how crucial communication is. Regardless, no matter how eloquent of a communicator you may be, it must be coming from a place of sincerity and substance for it to matter in a relationship. So, let's continue with your staple. Communication, both the spoken and the inferred, are crucial. For instance, if your partner tells you that you deserve better, despite it being flattering initially, you will also have to consider what would prompt your partner to say such as well as what he or she expects you to do with this information. Does it mean he or she is not that interested in you and a long-term commitment, or does it mean that he or she is admitting that he or she can do better and is encouraged by you simply being you? Find out as quickly as possible. Communication is not constant; it is always moving and should ideally be moving in the direction of your actions, as well as your partner's. Otherwise, you would be on opposing teams.

Earlier on in the chapter, I alluded to the pains and heartaches that arise from lack of preparation for a commitment, and it is clear how essential a role communication plays, especially when you are currently in some form of a relationship, as opposed to preparing yourself to go out there. Communication should be honest, so much so that it clears up any doubts or delusions your partner may have regarding anything in your relationship and who you are to each other as partners. Again, anything opposite to this means you spend time circling each other, wondering if, how and why when you are simply not compatible, and the soul mate for you is still out there. Consider sparing yourself and your partner the anxiety of not knowing how to think or what to do.

When I say *communication*, I understand that lying technically is classified as communication. The only controls you may have in your relationship where lying is concerned is for you to practice honesty as much as possible and share that you expect the same from your partner. You cannot force your partner to tell the truth, and you must be willing to admit to yourself first what your limits are about lying.

Relationships are like toddlers, requiring a lot of patience and attention to detail. The more details you ignore, the more likely it is that your relationship will be derailed. Sometimes, it is avoidable; other times, it is inevitable, based on how much preparation you put in and at what stage. Approach your relationship as one where you are constantly seeking to improve, as a toddler learns to walk, even after multiple painful tries and fails. At what point are you willing or prepared to give up on your relationship?

It has been proven, for me and others, that thoughts are more useful when shared, and communication is one avenue to do so. Preparation gives you and your partner a sense of direction and shared purpose. Keeping a relationship—a strong and mutually satisfying relationship, that is—takes hard work in real time; thinking things will just fall into place does a disservice to the potential of your relationship, not to mention the vested interest by your partner, and only increases frustration on both sides.

Invest in a friendship, and work on your relationship. Prioritize trust in your relationship. It takes years to build and only a minute to break or even shatter to near irreparable lengths. Opening yourself to a relationship means trusting, and that trust has to be earned over time, as you and your partner identify a shared goal and both worked positively to achieve this goal. Remember, wishful thinking alone does not make a relationship. Be prepared to put in the work, both on yourself and your partner. Any notion of successful relationships without work is false in my humble opinion. It takes dedication and devotion, from both partners.

Nothing is wrong with building on a friendship, if it includes years of tried and proven trust. Coming together is strong, which makes staying together more important.

2. QUESTION YOURSELF

This is such an underrated practice, yet it is so crucial when you are preparing for anything. Questioning yourself and your motives can lead you to make better decisions and better decision-making mechanisms. These questions should lead to more satisfactory decisions and taking care of details in between, like timing, being prepared, and ultimately, your approach in any decision. All these can be made easier by starting with answering those questions someone may ask of you if you were to justify your decisions.

Imagine being asked the why, and you don't have a convincing answer, much less having one altogether. How much less seriously would that person regard you, and how would he or she judge your level of commitment? This concept of introspection is not only applicable to intimate relationships but other relationships and experiences in one's life. The path to saying, "I do," will rigorously test you, in different ways. Often, we sidestep the fundamentals and instead embrace the unknown recklessly. I recommend a habit of approaching the mirror first to evaluate, before taking a step, any step.

Not only do you need to question yourself, but you also need to examine your concepts of anything and everything ultimately. Focusing on relationships, you must assess if your approach is positive or negative and why that would be so. It cannot be sugarcoated. You must be willing to see yourself for who you are and the stage you are at emotionally, physically, socially, spiritually, and financially. As we grow older, we change, form new ideas, and confirm our beliefs with our circumstances about who we are. Ultimately, having what I would call a concept of self is where an individual meets his or her thoughts and feelings, which, of course, makes it a prerequisite for premarital exploration.

Before I go any further, it is fair to confirm the conclusion you may have come to that I am from the old school because of the content of my text. However, I hope that my advice can be discerned past my generation. I do hope that most, if not all, readers can take away something relatable and practical. There is an old saying "Experience is a great teacher," which really means the longer you live, the more you can learn. I do hope that my experiences can offer some wisdom to you, having lived as I have so far, even though I wouldn't necessarily qualify as a peer to those generations after the baby boomers. I would test my limits and your patience possibly to dare say that based on observations, there are some children being raised by children in adult bodies. That is the raw truth, even admitted from some of these mouths, but I have digressed enough. Now it's back to the questions that you need to address.

The prerequisites to marriage, traditionally, are dating, courtship, and engagement. I would like to explore each as I have come to know them.

DATING

From a spiritual perspective, dating in the broadest sense means dating that is aligned with biblical principles or values, including nonsexual affection, as sex before marriage is unacceptable. However, I must contextualize how dating takes place without the Christian tenets, and hopefully, there should be some common ground.

Consider for a moment building a house. There are certain preparatory steps that one must take before mixing cement and laying bricks. You would need an architect to share the concept of your dream house and work through the details with you, even the seemingly insignificant ones. The architect would then translate your expressed requests into a vision, a blueprint, that would explain and facilitate the practicality and workability of your requests. Details like the best type of building material all at first seem to be no big deal, until they are. Similarly, the Bible has set the precedent to consider dating one of the preparatory steps before arriving at marriage.

Dating is usually further pulled apart by virtue of Christian precepts as opposed to the world's acceptable practices at large. In the Bible, for instance, there are fundamentals from which you can determine if you can take this dating to the next step. In 2 Corinthians 6:14–15 (NKJV), it says, "Do not be unequally yoked together with unbelievers. But what fellowship has the righteous with lawlessness and what communion has light with darkness?" In the context of these verses, the starkest contrast is set between believers and unbelievers. Likewise, such contrasts are usually evident from the dating stage. This could translate to a Christian woman not pursuing or entertaining the notion of a relationship with a non-Christian man and vice versa. It goes without saying that from a worldly perspective, the results would be a little different based on what one deems righteous and not righteous.

The Bible does not condone unequally yoked pairs, but our civilization, in contrast, widely accepts what we Christians would classify as unequally yoked relationships; this simply means such relationships are more prevalent, sadly, and sometimes, that minute lack of compatibility can lead to and has led to divorce. For a Christian believer, I do say that if you believe in the precepts and act contrary by disobeying the fundamental principles, then there will be consequences.

It is like being told of the fatal statistics of those who drive while texting or drunk, and yet you take the same risk, without accepting the possibility of the same fatal response. Regardless, believers and nonbelievers alike need to pay attention to what the fundamentals are, as soon as possible, while dating. As a believer myself, when I am self-questioning, I usually compare my thoughts with what the spiritual expectations are as laid out in the Bible. That forms part of my compass; nevertheless, that also means, generally, we must be conscious of the fact that it may be to our detriment if we do the opposite of what our beliefs have convicted in us to be the right thing, which is God's plan for the institution of marriage. For those of my readers who are nonbelievers, whatever that compass is, find it.

Another aspect of dating that I consider dangerous that is also prevalent is having sex on the same night you meet someone or a few days after that meeting. The traditionalist in me, as well as my beliefs personally, do not classify this as dating in that it only addresses one aspect of dating. Remember dating, which should not necessarily be drawn out either, is where two people socialize with the aim of evaluating each other's suitability as partners. Of course, the topic of intimacy will come up in due course.

Dating is not the attachment from the get-go phase. You can literally take some time to discover, while you work on yourself. Of course, after mentally and emotionally preparing for the concept and committing to putting in the work, you should also, in this phase, ask questions as soon as something causes a crease in your eyebrows.

Granted, I do observe a little—okay, a lot—of impatience in just how society approaches some things. Because dating should be the precursor to marriage, it is warranted that you take the time, invest in it even. Every stage is important.

To err on the side of caution, on the first date at least, I would recommend delaying the kissing, petting, touching, and sharing of certain confidential information, which is important of course for security reasons also. One question to ask yourself is whether you are prepared to share any information and what you are comfortable with sharing. That is just my recommendation. Other scenarios that you should consider are if you find yourself in a secluded spot with your date, how would you react? What would you do if he or she showed up with a friend? Are you confident in yourself? Your date can also discern that—especially a date who has nefarious intentions and is emotionally intelligent enough to manipulate you.

Do you know the voice and tone of your gut instinct, and would you be in tune with it? If your date asks you about where you are from, what you do, and so on, how much information are you prepared to give him or her? I always say give no more than what already exists on the internet, although in some cases, that is already too much information. That information poses security risks to you on account of people who may have ill intentions. Are you willing to put your security on the line? How do you feel about your date being long-term unemployed, and I am not speaking of unemployment as a result of COVID-19? Would you be willing to heed advice if your mentor should point out any observations to you?

All the above are part and parcel in the dating realm, and it is best to have a concept of what may happen and have a hypothetical plan for a few scenarios.

Also, it is not unfamiliar to my generation to date multiple partners; for the most part, initially, dating is more social than intimate, as we evaluate each other. This contrast is one I must come to terms with: dating doesn't mean the same for everyone. Some view dating as a commitment of sorts, and thus the entitlements and the expectations are clear. Are you prepared for such a partner and to navigate any potential conflict?

At any stage of your dating experience, have you considered how you would respond to being disrespected, especially in public or in front of your friends or family? What would you even classify as disrespect? The probabilities exist. How do you feel about your date and recreational drugs?

Having tried to engage the congregation at different ages as well as non-Christian youth, I would try to understand the appeal of great security risks and such dating experiences, and I would wonder if that was what the '50s or '60s is best regarded for. This is usually a popular retort when certain observations are made to this target group.

All I must ask is this: have you considered the possibilities, and if so, have you decided how you are prepared to act?

Which then brings me to…

COURTSHIP

This biblical definition of courtship is when both partners prayerfully and purposefully seek to determine if a marriage between them is a part of God's grand plan for their lives. For believers, that conviction is essential. Courtship follows dating after a period and after certain prerequisites have been satisfied. Courtship usually successfully precedes an engagement. The main distinction between the two is the level of causality and the level of commitment. Courtship means increased commitment. Courtship is always where a declaration would have been made that both partners expect to stay together and work on themselves as independent humans but also as a unit exclusively. Courtship is where a certain level of discernment would have been arrived at, to say that the time and energies invested have a shared long-term goal, leading to marriage. It is the time when the pretenses are usually tired, and the true person comes through, as pretense is the enemy of a relationship built on the values of trust and reciprocity. No well-meaning long-term relationship has any purpose for neglect rather than to weed it out, as quickly as possible. There is no space in a well-meaning relationship for the partners involved to suffer pain and anguish in silence.

Remember, courtship is not marriage, but it is supposed to get you that much closer. And at either the stage of dating or courtship, if there are any irreconcilable differences that come as a surprise, then there is no failure in an amicable parting of ways. Are you prepared at any point to listen to your instincts and walk away, even if you feel invested?

Engagement and marriage do not mean that any of your unresolved issues from courtship will be automatically and magically solved—only that more time has passed, and there has been no solution. Consider having major disagreements, disagreements based on your agreed limits, during courtship, and they remain unresolved, because there is no active search for or application of a solution. That relationship would most likely fall apart as the transition in and of itself does not provide any solution. That remains something that you must actively work on. All that means is that you have now said, "I do," with this elephant in the room. That does a disservice to you and your partner.

And finally, one of the questions being asked as it relates to relationships and courtship is how long it should last. I know I mentioned that no stage should be drawn out, but there is no scripted answer. It depends on many factors and the partners involved. The courtship will directly be impacted by the level of maturity displayed by its members.

On my radio show, I like to remind my listeners that marriage is for a certain level of maturity, after the transition from boy or girl to man or woman. Maturity is where the difference is. It is not just about your physicality but your mental awareness and your ability to deliberate on decisions. These factors will impact how long you court for. Also, the age of both partners, as age, by virtue of experiences, may have a role to play in the level of maturity that is expected as a relationship progresses. Statistically, older partners may find less need for a longer- term courtship as opposed to the other way around.

One thing is for certain: both parties should have a sense of belonging as they transition to the next stage, which is engagement.

ENGAGEMENT

Engagement or betrothal occurs when the relationship has developed overtime, and marriage is the next goal. Traditionally, the man would propose to the woman before her family, which can be an exciting time for parents to witness. During your introspection, as you question yourself, do you consider engagement, or even marriage, the final stop? As in you are safe now?

Most Christian counselors discourage long engagements because of the uncertainty of remaining free from sexual immorality. Even though Paul wrote this to single Christians, it was mostly to engaged couples: "To the unmarried and the widows, I say to remain unmarried as I am, but if they cannot exercise self-control, they should marry. For it is better to marry than to burn with passion" (1 Corinthians 7:8–9 NKJV).

A ceremony usually commemorates such a step and the much-anticipated gesture of putting the ring on the woman's finger. This gesture is intended to symbolize a lifetime commitment and reflect the beauty of the relationship that begets it. Furthermore, the ring is circular, which can also symbolize interconnectedness and having no end separate from the beginning or how people are brought together in a serendipitous way.

Wearing the ring on the left figure is a gesture steeped in history, stemming from the Romans, who believed that the left hand contained a vein that ran directly to the heart, dubbing it *vena amorist*, or vein of love. One would say wearing the ring on this hand and finger symbolized love and affairs of the heart, both of which should be present in those who walk this path. Conversely, today's wearing of a ring in some instances is no longer just about love but making a statement of stature and possession, of signaling victory to perceived rivals for the affections of the man, since it is most usually the men who propose.

With this part of the journey realized and transitioning into the next, here are a few things that both parties should invest the time to discuss:

1. Partners must pledge a never-ending love affair with each other.
2. Partners must discuss the topic of family planning, and it must be laid on the table. Each partner must express his or her thoughts on the subject, while maintaining respect for the other's. The aim is a mutually beneficial solution.
3. Partners must categorize long-term and short-term goals.

4. Partners must discuss, in further detail, their finances. When in doubt, it is safest for both to open a joint account and discuss the terms of that account.
5. Partners' financial ambitions must not be neglected, and so various sorts of investments must be discussed here.
6. Lifestyle choices must also be discussed, including certain practices such as smoking and drinking. Some of this should ideally be done during courtship, but at this stage, engagement would be the final stop before the next chapter.
7. Self-development also should be discussed as partners should continuously work on themselves.
8. Again, once the topic of family planning has been agreed on, the next step is to decide where you would like to raise this family, if it is separate from where you both are now.
9. Partners should discover each other's love language and discuss certain important components, such as affirmation, quality time, gift-giving, physical intimacy, and anticipating your partner's needs.
10. Partners should also discuss the topic of religion and how they intend to include God in their marriage.

One of the most unforgettable moments for me was on my wedding day. I was transfixed by my wife, all innocent and gorgeous. The feeling alone was like being on cloud nine, as after being single for many years, I was convinced I had finally come home to the woman destined for me. Proverbs 18:22 (NKJV) declares, "He who finds a wife, finds a good thing." On this premise, my wife became my treasure and my queen, and she has so remained for thirty-three years now.

Granted, there were unavoidable bumps in our marital journey, but those were resolved quickly.

Navigating each other's likes and dislikes was and remains an interesting experience. Dating and living together were two separate things we realized, or maybe one just exposed more about us and our habits, like taking off shoes wherever or talking nonstop. Simple things. Now as soon as you live together, this is where the rubber meets the road.

This is the time for both partners to find out if the other was pretending to seem unfazed for the most part during dating. These series of revelations, I call them tests, reveal much about the character and moral standing of each person. It will uncover the strength of one's capacity to love, like, or dislike. It will reveal much about one's morals and ethics, thus approximating the life span of one's marriage.

I have accepted that no marriage is perfect, and it is no reason to be dismayed, as it depends on your definition of *perfect*. One component that is crucial is how you and your partner disagree. Sometimes, depending on the topic, you may have to agree to disagree. At least that way, you would see the credence of Amos 3:3, which says, "How can two walk together except they be agreed?" Husbands and wives need to forgive one another after the confrontation is over, work out the differences, and move on. The enemy will enter your hearts if you continue to dwell on the same issues.

Whenever my wife and I experience a misunderstanding, especially when we must agree to disagree, we usually allow our passions to cool off and then seek counsel through prayer. Then, with a prayerful heart, we reassess the issues between us. The solutions are not always fully satisfactory for both parties. But we learn from our lessons. For instance, I was always encouraged not to take the bills of the house lightly, and yet I did not heed that advice. My neglect on the same matter ended up costing us thousands of dollars. Paying attention to details is important.

Historically, marriage was embraced by all in ancient history, Christians and non-Christians alike, as well as Hebrews, Greeks, and Romans, having been first recorded around by BC. Since the institution of marriage predates traditional Christianity, such as Abrahamic religions, Judaism and Islam, which shared common origins and values. It needs recognition by all.

Marriage is an eclectic collection of practices and beliefs, but God, the Creator of all, regardless of time, did declare in Genesis 2:24 (NKJV), "Therefore a man shall leave his father and mother and be joined to his wife, and they shall become one flesh." This was reaffirmed by Jesus in Matthew 19:4–6 (NKJV) with "And he answered and said unto them 'Have you not read that He who made them at the beginning made them male and female and said for this reason a man shall leave his father and mother and be joined to his wife and the two shall become one flesh. So then, they are no longer two but one flesh. Therefore, what God has joined together, let no man separate."

Genesis 2:4 (NKJV) is the foundation of the biblical adoption of marriage. Since in marriage, a man is to leave his family, join his wife, and unite with her, this establishes that a new, distinct home is to be made, separate from the parents. It does not sever any ties with family but creates an extended family, which by all accounts, was close-knit and interdependent.

In this verse, the term "be joined" refers to a marital bond, symbolic of a union. Man was instructed to cleave to his wife and leave his parents' home. Based on observations, men, for the most part, do not take kindly to this part of the instruction. Instead, the practice is to take their wives home to their parents as opposed to away. I prefer to err on the side of the total symbolism of not only putting a ring on my wife's finger but also to make a new home for us, unattached to that of my parents or her parents. It is always good to take the initiative, without being prompted, but, of course, a blessed man is one who has the support of his wife.

If you are at that stage in your life, you are encouraged to question everything I just described. You intend to be joined to this man or woman. What does *be joined* mean to you? And how far are you prepared to go with this relationship or marriage?

3. AM I REALLY READY FOR A RELATIONSHIP?

A profound question and deliberation to undertake is that of "Am I ready for a relationship?" It is best to not answer prematurely. When preparing for a relationship, on the self-introspection journey, this question must be dissected separately. The questioning of one as an individual existing within the society must exist without the involvement of a rclationship. But now, let us examine some of the intricacies of a relationship. You need to do a thorough evaluation of yourself in the context of a relationship, maturity, sense of responsibility, commitment, habits, temperament, religious beliefs, and something called timing. Falling in love happens when it does, but how do you really know that you are in love? I tell you what: it certainly does not happen overnight, and incorrect timing can lead to the premature demise of a relationship.

Some overlooked aspects of the readiness assessment are how much you know about your partner and assessing the flow of the relationship so far away from your partner. Only men who are concerned with their future will want to ask if they are ready for a relationship, if they are ready to say, "I do." In retrospect, I did not ask myself this question, but I was getting older, and fortunately for me, my partner was a Christian believer. One of my favorite verses is Psalm 37:4 (NKJV): "Delight yourself in the Lord, and He shall give you the desires of your heart." I want to say emphatically that this scripture came to pass for me in a spectacular way, and this is the only safe way of foregoing the readiness assessment.

Instead of me asking my truest self if I was ready for a relationship, I was told through the Holy Spirit that I was ready. So instead of a question, what I experienced was a revelation. I was instructed by God to fast and pray for my wife, after God revealed to me that I was ready. So, I got a revelation and instructions. Thankfully, I heeded them. I obeyed. For believers, it is crucial to understand that God does not stereotype. He will speak to each of us once we present ourselves to him in earnestly. As believers, we must be present and willing to heed God's instructions.

Another key toward readiness is responsibilities. The very definition of *responsibility* is something that is required to be done, as part of a job, a role, or a legal obligation. Responsibility can also be viewed as collaborative since marriage is between two people. Collaborative responsibility is what accounts for the wins as well as the shortfalls in a marriage. If there is a win, it is shared by both, and conversely, if there is a loss, it is absolved by both. I mentioned earlier that because of my neglect in paying attention to our bills, there was a cost of thousands of dollars spent trying to correct that mistake. That cost, loss, affected us as a family unit, because of my neglect. Marriage is teamwork. It helps when both partners have the same goal and the same vision behind that goal.

Being responsible should be a state of mind and not just a flippant feeling or one associated with some things. Responsibility must become a part of who you are evolving into, as you continue to work on yourself. If one considers marriage as a relationship goal, responsibility should be a default state of being, and you must be prepared to be a constant support for your wife, regardless of the time or tide, good or bad. This is where you are introduced to endurance, especially if children are already in the picture or are coming into the picture.

When contemplating if you are ready for a relationship, you must be willing to be honest about your track record in commitment. How are you dedicating for the long term, even when there is no clear or near reward that you can see? It will require you to have an open conversation with your partner about being committed to putting in the work in the relationship, to being open, honest, forgiving, understanding, and supportive and striving to always be so. You may not always achieve it, but at least you will strive toward it. Simply be present for the people you care for.

Some men like to play blame/shame at their partner's expense, all to cover up an attitude of lack of commitment. It's a very dangerous game to be a part of, especially without the knowledge that you are being played. Are you ready to deal with the situation if you find that your spouse constantly and purposely says things to provoke you? It can happen to anyone. Jean-Paul Barter said, "Commitment is an action, not words." Are you ready to actively discern between the two? Between questioning yourself and really trying to assess if you are ready for a relationship, these are some of the questions that you should be asking and some of the scenarios that you should be hypothesizing.

The truth is relationships without commitments have no depth. Proverbs 16:3 (NKJV) says, "Commit thy works unto the Lord and thy thoughts shall be established." The Lord expects us to be committed to Him and each other, always, regardless of the circumstances. Commitment is one of the building blocks for a successful relationship. Commitment is needed for laying the foundation on which successful relationships are built. Commitment is what drives loyalty as opposed to disloyalty in relationships, and sometimes, it is painfully obvious.

Every strong family begins with a committed man, which I will analogize with a house foundation. The strength of a house lies upon the foundation. If the foundation is weak, then the entire building is vulnerable and thus easily compromised. Conversely, a solid foundation begets a durable house. Since every component depends on a durable foundation, it also means that the longevity of that house depends on the foundation. In this way, the entire family depends on the man to be that strong and not an easily shaken foundation. To all my male readers, are you ready to be the foundation of your family? To be relied upon for that unwavering support?

Another key aspect of relationship readiness is maturity. Maturity is defined as the state of fully developed adulthood, capable of deliberating to make the best decisions and exercising good judgment. Six qualities by which to evaluate your maturity are the following:

1. Possessing a spirit of humility, which is usually accomplished through the greatest examples of servanthood. It then requires all to have and maintain an attitude of servitude, especially with regard to the context of a relationship. Are you ready to serve your partner? Male or female? To make it more relatable, only a humble person would see an opportunity of servitude coming out of listening to the concerns of their partners, even while they themselves navigate personal distresses. Are you ready for that? Humility will require patience and tolerance; Humility means not feeling the least bit insecure about the attention your partner is getting. This is why arrogance is its opposite. In arrogance, one seeks the attention for oneself. Are you ready to call it as you see it? Humble or arrogant? A humble person has the capacity to love at a rating of eight or nine out of ten, whereas an arrogant person's capacity peaks at about four. A mature man is not consumed with drawing attention to himself but rather to his partner. He would be consumed by his partner and vice versa.

2. Maturity means decision-making is not based solely on feelings but on character, the character of a person upon assessing a situation. Character means integrity, what one does when no one is watching, expecting, or critiquing. A mature person can appreciate that character in a person. Are you ready to

communicate the importance of character in your relationship? If not, then there should be no rush in the relationship until you have both decided to work on yourself and each other. This prevents avoidable chaos for both you and your intended partner. Maturity means that even though you validate your emotions, you are predominantly guided by your false sense of security in your decision-making. Your values are never compromised, so that if all else fails, you can still stay true to your values.

3. Mature people seek sagacity before acting. They are not ashamed to seek counsel, especially from those more experienced on the subject at hand. They depend on friends and family whom they have in their inner circle for this on-hand counsel, or if they are like me, they rely on God Almighty. James 1:5 NKJV declares, "If any of you lacks wisdom, let him ask God, who gives to all, liberally and without reproach." A mature man does not presume to have all the answers but instead is open to more succinct reasoning. Admittedly the wiser a person gets, the more he or she seeks wisdom. Wisdom is a staple in long-term successful relationships.

4. Mature people consistently and sincerely express their gratitude. Gratitude is the highest form of appreciation to God for all that He has done. Mature people express gratitude for the partner they have been given, especially if they are convicted they have been given that partner by God. Mature people show gratitude for being united with their spouse, and it speaks volumes. Melody Beattie said, "Gratitude makes sense of our past, brings peace for today, and creates a vision for tomorrow."

5. Mature people do not shy away from long-term commitments. They would have known what they wanted and having been granted what they sought would seek to keep it for as long as they could. My listeners from my bi-monthly podcasts show can always confirm that I give timely reminders that long-term commitments, especially for marriages, are not for fleet spirits or the faint of heart, meaning, not for boys and girls or

teenagers, who have shorter attention spans when it comes to planning and embracing the future. Maturity is what will make you at peace with investing time, money, and emotional support into a partner.

6. Mature people do not abandon the family they have made or chosen to make. Abandonment, which is more prevalent than we think, usually starts sometime before the divorce. Divorce is typically the result of long-term abandonment. So instead of mutual, long-term commitment, one partner abandons the other. This is the result of a relationship that was not founded on maturity, trust, and wisdom, for starters. You must ask yourself if you have it in you to suddenly abandon your relationship and on what grounds, especially when times get hard? More so, are you ready to deal with yourself after you have been abandoned? I cannot emphasize enough the importance of preparation.

Based on my assignment, being in the field of relationship counselor, our men of today are not adequately prepared for the transition from singlehood to married life. It seems like a game instead of a conscious and transformative journey. In some cases, this is only the case for one of the partners, when one has expressed and qualified that he or she is committed and ready, and the next partner appears to just be fishing.

For men especially, here are a few things to consider before contemplating saying "I do."

The number one symbol of being single is freedom. Not to say there will not be freedom in a commitment, but there is more emphasis on commitment and responsibility. For instance, some things that you would do as a single person may not be applicable in a committed relationship. Depending on what the habit is, it may seem inhibitive and restrictive. You must discuss the limits and boundaries with your partner. What would you do if you and your partner cannot agree on some of these limits and boundaries? It is something to consider. You must be open and honest with yourself, but more importantly, you must be willing to compromise.

After self-introspection and exploring the other areas of preparedness, you will ultimately be able to determine if you are ready or not. Cognitively and behaviorally, you will feel the shift in your consciousness, as you now commit to primarily being responsible for someone else and someone else being responsible for you, if that is the commitment intended. That shift in mindset is tantamount to transcending; however, despite some partners in expected committed relationships, the behavior clashes, as it reflects that single mindedness continues to prevail. Apostle Paul declares in 1 Corinthians 13:11 (NJKV), "When I was a child, I spoke as a child, I understood as a child, I thought as a child. But when I became a man, I put away childish things."

Sadly, the reality is not many potential partners get this concept. I have witnessed attempts by some to be married and at the same time do things a single person would. In fact, they have a family at home, waiting on them, praying for their safe return, yet these men, for some reason, want to live a double life and expect everything to be fine with all parties involved. That would be the truest case of compartmentalization if I have ever seen one, and I have not so far. It escapes these men that respect goes two ways, and it must start with them.

It also seems incomprehensible to grasp for many men that simply lusting after the opposite sex, in an uncontrolled and reckless manner. Matthew 5:28 (NKJV) states, "But I say unto you, whoever looks at a woman lust for her has already committed adultery with her in his heart." The word *lust* is defined to have a strong sexual desire for someone. This means a man does not need to have sexual intercourse to commit adultery or fornication. Just looking at her with sexual intentions from his heart, he commits a sin.

Lust can be destructive for both male and female factors, especially while you may be consumed with the very thought of fulfilling this strong urge without any regards for one's feelings or emotions. This includes, how the opposite sex would receives your advances as you express your lust that should cause you to dismay, this could be destructive to both male and female factors. The inability to control one's lust can lead to socially unacceptable actions, violations, and unethical behaviors, such as rape, simply because one has not learned to control one's urges.

The saying by Napoleon Hill, "Whatever you perceive, you can achieve," explains the power of the mind and the reckless consequences of not controlling and taking responsibility for that mind. Your thoughts can permeate your entire being and guide your actions, consciously or subconsciously. One's thoughts are always to be kept in check. It speaks to other issues, such as character and approachability; when our young men are not able to do anything other than fixate on their lust, feeding there obsession with thoughts with their minds. Add that amount of immaturity and lack of impulse control with ill intentions, place women on the list of prey by men who have no good intentions and are all amped up on unchecked lust.

In this time is one when almost everything is on display. All the tears in our social fabric are evident, as is the subsequent damage. It is all painful, especially in this time. Are you ready for a relationship right now? What if your partner reveals details about his or her past actions that do not sit comfortably with you? How do you navigate those conversations? Are you ready for that discomfort, in the name of pursuing a long-term commitment?

Side note: it cannot go unsaid anymore other than to groom the next generation properly, how else do we engender a sense of law and order and civic responsibility in our people, particularly our men? How do we allow for the revelation that youth speak with a certain level of immaturity or lack of respect generally to balance with a corrective measure that is both progressive and also rehabilitative? Respect goes both ways by default, so those who expect respect must also act with respect first and foremost. It is essential to point out that relationships are all around us, in many forms, as we are social creatures, and thus we must be ready for the manifestations of our relationships but also of others' relationships.

Are you ready to tackle a relationship in which it appears your significant other prefers to be referred to as a sugar daddy as opposed to a partner?

Are you willing to walk away, if necessary, from your sugar daddy and, if so, under what circumstances? Granted, sometimes sugar daddies only masquerade as such on account of being too busy as a CEO or some such executive for the work required for a long-term commitment. This is the only drawback as they spend lavishly on their dates. Are you prepared to handle such a proposal? It becomes even harder when these men do open up and share that at some point in the past, lifestyle or not, they had opened up and were hurt. Are you ready for such complexities?

I have heard much, including that a trustworthy woman is a dead one, meaning once a woman has breath in her body, then she cannot be trusted wholeheartedly. Of course, I discourage such utterances, but that statement is made from a place of hurt, where no logic resides. Of course, there are two sides to every story, but who has the time to put both parties in the same room to hash out whatever contention exists, and how will we fully verify as an observer, when we weren't there? Basically, take things with a grain of salt. Are you ready for a conversation that requires discernment?

Are you ready to accept that no matter how much good you do, one misstep can completely dislodge the trust and reciprocity in your relationship? Are you ready, in any relationship that you have, to accept the loss of relationships you hold dear based on a mistake that you have made or suffered after speaking your truth? There is no one fix for a relationship; nor is there one rubric. There are only guiding concepts. How it plays out is between you and your partner. So, are you ready?

Moving on.

In any relationship, when it comes to kindness, it never hurts to continue being kind, even when the relationship has dissolved. How you exit a relationship speaks volumes to your level of maturity prior to the relationship and after its ending. It never hurts to remain cordial with a person after the fact, as kindness is unforgettable, and the person will always regard you well. Personally, not one of my previous friends would ever say I was unkind, because that was not the case. Years later, if we meet by chance, there is a sense of camaraderie between us.

In case the preceding scenarios only answer some of your concerns about being ready for a relationship, here are a few more:

1. You have concluded that you are ready. You are ready for a relationship when you accept that you are now ready to be included in new experiences with another person, ready to do things you have never done and see things you have never seen with this person. You are looking to share yourself and your love with someone else, as opposed to just getting love.

2. You chose a like-minded partner. This essentially means someone who mirrors your beliefs, preferences, and ambitions. This level of like-mindedness translates to compatibility, which is crucial in deliberating on a lifelong partner. Compatibility helps chart the course in marriages, since both partners are on the same path, especially when it comes to making certain pertinent decisions. This means fewer clashes in making decisions as a unit. Others have angst that comes from incompatibility, which is what I would now like to contrast.

Incompatibility means that the two are even sometimes opposite of each other. When one likes something, the other may not. It is as simple as that. It starts and may chart the path to graver disagreements. Please avoid this pitfall. Again, I pull for the scripture in Amos 3:3 (NKJV): "Can two walk together except they agree?" The operative word here is *agree*. Without a sense of agreement, conflict is inevitable, unavoidable, and almost always detrimental and irreparable.

Agreeing means having harmony or accordance in an opinion or feeling. If there is no agreement, then there is no compatibility, and disagreements will then be more regular than agreements, starting a toxic trend within your relationship. Are you prepared for navigating this cycle?

3. You have exhausted your search. A wise person would explore all options and give him- or herself time to do so. You must

use all tools available, including time, to find the best-suited partner for you based on your basic requirements. You have to come to this realization before declaring that you are ready for a relationship, because the work starts with the search. The results can either make you or break you. It is advisable that you spend the time and invest in the search, which can be long and arduous; however, it is less so than committing prematurely, especially if your search's sole purpose is to lead to a long-term partner.

In short, there is no clear-cut answer as to how long this process will take, as it depends on what you are looking for, where you are looking, and what you are willing to accept. Rather than fixating on how long the process will take, I would recommend instead painting a visual aid of what you are looking for in this partner you seek.

4. Lastly, you would not settle for feelings of infatuation. Infatuation is when you are falling in love with someone in a short time. People often mistake infatuation for love. It is not the same, because the feeling of infatuation doesn't last long. Love is a deep affection for someone, affection that has been tested by time and remains standing. Love searches deeper than the surface and deepens the intimacy and spiritual connection that two may have. That process does not take place overnight.

True love searches the heart and the intentions of the person prior to its manifestation.

Falling in love immediately, especially in our modern society, is a recipe for disaster, pain, and misfortune. There is an old saying "don't gamble with love, its only for fools." So settling for a relationship that you are not sure is solid or living daily with the hope that it will become solid is likened to being a fool. When you are at the point close to closing the deal, you must see the person's heart not with your physical eyes but with your own heart—that is, love.

Infatuation in relationships is one of the leading causes of pitfalls in marriages. It is antilove and antiromance, with a short life span to match. It is a misfortune that plagues people with good intentions. Overcoming infatuation is very difficult, especially when you are playing games. Overcoming infatuation begins with replacing those thoughts with reality.

Purpose will help you analyze the person's faults and behavioral patterns, which is more important in the infatuation phase. All an infatuated person can think is how perfect the person he or she is infatuated with is. A reality check would make you realize and accept that no one is perfect, and then you can refocus on things in your partner that really matter to you and the prosperity of the relationship. If all else fails, you can seek professional help, because you may be doing the right thing at to the wrong time or even with the wrong person.

Assessing if you are ready for a relationship is key, and it only does good for your relationship to assess before making any long-term commitments. I say, face both yourself and your reality head-on as soon as possible if you want your relationship to prosper.

4. WHY DO I THINK THAT I AM READY?

It is important to ponder if one is ready for relationship and be ready to justify this conviction of relatonship readiness.

I purposefully addressed contemplating one's readiness for marriages before questioning that contemplation, because that is predominantly what needs to happen.

While we explored some of the scenarios that you may encounter being in a relationship, you may have fully answered yes to some of them, meaning that, yes, you are ready. This is now the space where I help you answer for yourself why you think you are ready, and that must be good enough.

Being ready must start with you, preferably unencumbered by poor decision-making tactics or even external commentary. This journey you will take with your to-be partner is a journey for both of you, at least in the first instance, so it is a momentous decision, much more than a passing thought or just a reaction to a scenario. I will delve into it. Essentially, you need to respond from a place of conviction, where as little doubt as possible resides.

You need to have a strong case and a robust conviction of assuring yourself that you are ready for what may lie ahead, based on what you have assessed you are looking for, that is the only way you would be able to convince your partner to take this journey with you. And yes, having a strong start by being ready and prepared goes a long way to ensuring longevity and success in the endeavor. In this case, it is a relationship or long-term commitment.

I refer to 1 Corinthians 10:12 (NKJV), which states, "Therefore let him who thinks he stands, take heed lest he falls." This simply means that we need a constant evaluation of our standing to ensure more times than not that we can keep our footing despite the circumstances. When I refer to strength in this context, more important than physical strength is mental strength, which requires having discipline over your mind and its constant fluctuations. You must be able to reach for what is important, whenever you need to and as quickly as you need to. Training your mind in these ways also qualifies as being ready.

Let's go back to the transition, where you are currently single and are asking yourself to justify your readiness for a relationship.

Singleness, by law, is defined as a state of not being married. Often, to escape "single doom," we tend to latch all our hopes and fantasies on the first potential partner we see, which is not only unfair to us but also to this person. Single men do not think about settling down, especially in the prime of life, and date multiple partners to suit their own egos. Take me, for instance. Before I was uber-ready and prostrated myself in supplication before God, ready to heed His instructions, I too gallivanted about. In my early twenties, I would party with the best of them and date multiple partners, because that was the concept of being single and I had no intentions yet of readying myself for a relationship.

It was my time in the army that gave me some semblance of structure, for beginners. I had to take care of my appearance, from my hair to my boots and everything in between. If I recall, the ladies were very appreciative of this get-up, and it boosted my ego to some degrees. Everything was going great in singledom, as that was the only thing that I was technically ready for, until I had to go to a party that one of my friends was told not to go to. At three thirty in the morning, I discovered that my friend had died after an altercation with a young man. I was crushed, and at the same time, I considered that it could easily have been me. I tell you all of that to say that knowing what I do now, if I had known it then, I would have acted differently.

Thinking on it now, I can easily see how things go wrong once there is an opportunity for them to go wrong. What's more, when I was in my twenties, most of the advice I garnered came through my peers as opposed to my parents. My dad was an avid worker, and he did so for long hours each day. By the time he got home, my siblings and I were asleep. My mother also tried to counsel me. I did not heed her. Come to think of it, had I heeded her advice, things would have gone differently, a lot of things. What I did not know was that my mother's advice was certainly to prepare me for long-term commitments, not just intimate relationships but also friendships. Yet, I clung to the sole advisory group of my peers. Suffice it to say, that did not prepare me much for the long-term commitments that I sought.

Most of our young men are looking for young ladies who are vulnerable, young women who are desperate for any relationship they can find. This scenario most times would soon enough land these men with a pregnant girlfriend. Clearly the missing element in this scenario is sound counseling on what makes a long-term relationship and what makes it work.

I dare to suggest to every young man at this stage in his life that he should not hesitate to start thinking about and planning and preparing for his future. If you are like me, always relying heavily on the Word of God, let me assure you that it contains much advice and wisdom points that we can all draw from. Specifically, to the edification of our young people, Proverbs 3:10 (NKJV) says, "Do not be wise in your own eyes, fear the Lord and depart from evil"—emphasis on the words *fear* and *Lord*. Fear means to respect the authority and wisdom of the Lord, the first counselor. For every young person who seeks the Lord and wisdom, especially for counsel in his or her long-term relationship, this is a good start. Once you acknowledge and fear God, then you will begin to see the same approach to yourself and those around you.

Another scripture to further drive home the question and the encouraged quest to test if you are really ready is Proverbs 1:7 (NKJV), which says, "The fear of the Lord is the beginning of knowledge, but fools despise wisdom and instructions." It simply means that wisdom does not exist in a vacuum; wherever you seek it, it is accompanied by heeding instructions. For all believers, any healthy introspection must start with having a fear of God.

This enlightenment will truly reveal whether believers are really at the place of maturity that they originally thought.

Once you have a clearer understanding of fear of the Lord, it is easier to work on your loyalty, as this will be crucial in a relationship. You must be ready for loyalty even when it is not returned, and the best place to start is with the Word of God, which teaches all things. Loyalty plays a role in each relationship, and the fact is, there are some relationships that will take longer to reach that secure place of loyalty than others.

Loyalty in any relationship and to anyone is not a sprint. Sometimes, it is a marathon or a decathlon, especially since it also works closely with trust. Loyalty tells your partner how much you care for him or her. Loyalty has to do within the feeling of your support and duty toward your partner. Being supportive of your partner will create a sense of security and safety, which is only good for your relationship.

Have you asked yourself about your readiness for a relationship? If you answered yes with much confidence, what exactly was your answer on loyalty and trust? Are they conditional? If so, what are your terms?

Lack of these essentials, especially if you are being honest with yourself, results in insecurity. Once that takes root in your relationship, it is hard to uproot. Do you think you are ready to be that constant support to your partner, especially when it is about building trust and encouraging loyalty to each other? For believers who have been conditioned to be the weaker vessels, it is then the responsibility of the man to be able to offer his support, be that strength, and bear the weight without falling apart and without complaint.

A loyal partnership also has integrity, and this should be engendered in the relationship from as early out as possible. Integrity means you are doing the right thing for yourself and your partner, even when no one is watching. Integrity means being careful not to devalue your character or that of your partner. Integrity translates to value, value placed on you, your partner, and your relationship.

Integrity does not mean that mistakes won't happen. It is about how you admit to those mistakes and encourage corrective behaviors that speak to any regret you may have, especially if it causes pain to your partner. Integrity in a relationship also means that there will be a sense of pride in the love, attention, commitment, support, and devotion to your partner. It is especially crucial when you are considering saying, "I do," to this person.

A person of integrity is sensitive and accountable to his or her partner. Such people are kind and respectful of their own values and those of their partners. They respect boundaries. Marriages fall apart without integrity and commitment—commitment to the person you are about to say "I do" to or the person you have already said "I do" to.

Loyalty also requires sincerity, even in the most random acts of support and compassion. It shows unending commitment to your partner. It takes the form of deeds and words, which are also often overlooked. James 5:16 (NKJV) declares, "Confess your faults to one another, that you may be healed." What does that mean? Sometimes it means speaking the truth, which may not be what your partner wants to hear. The truth ultimately should heal, and since you are committed to your partner, it means you are also committed to his or her healing, as well as yours.

Now that you have an idea of some of the questions to ask yourself about yourself and not necessarily what you are ready for in a partner, it is time to address some of the uncomfortable ones or the least talked about ones.

One is your credit score. Another incontestable piece of evidence that signals your readiness to say "I do" is credit. A good credit score means you are debt free, and this is essential, especially if your spouse wants to have a family. Do not get me wrong: having manageable credit is also good, but ideally being debt free is more attractive, especially if you or your partner are particular about this detail. It means more financial security and a certain degree of certainty in the relationship. Are you prepared to disclose your credit if asked by your partner? Are you also prepared to address a less-than-ideal credit for either yourself or your partner?

I emphasize having healthy credit does not stand alone; however, it is a signal of the financial prospects of having liquid assets. So, treat your credit with respect and as a sign of being ready for some semblance of financial commitment and stability. Do not be offended if a woman says she will have to consider being with a partner whose credit or financial standing leaves much to be desired. There must be some other redeemable quality of this partner.

If you are asking that of any woman, it means you expect women, or even men for that matter, to commit to financially unstable relationships. And by financially unstable, I do not mean to enduring a crisis like this pandemic but being able to withstand some amount of emergency spending without going bankrupt. Considering, statistically, that a lot of households already live paycheck to paycheck, why do you think you are ready for that eventuality, without further due diligence?

Answer honestly.

A symbol of being ready to say "I do" is financial stability or being somewhere on the spectrum. Having some sort of financial plan is one of those things that does not singlehandedly make a relationship but can singlehandedly break a relationship. Let that sink in.

In our society, too many of our young ladies are allowing men who are financially embarrassed to lower them into relationships or situations that are unsustainable. Interestingly, also, there are some men who do not wish to remain single despite not having the financial stability that is required for a long-term relationship. They would rather prey on young women who are also looking for love in all the wrong places.

There are a lot of pieces involved in being prepared for the final step; however, resources abound.

Something as simple as training your train of thought for the transition can be a big help. Your train of thought means a collection of thoughts and ideas, sometimes for a specific purpose and other times, multiple purposes. The bottom line is you have the power bank, and that is your mind. Now you can see the credence behind training your mind into more positive thoughts, and conversely, if one is reacting negatively to an already negative situation, then it may culminate in further evil yet calculated actions. I say again, the mind is that powerful, but it is yours, so you can train it.

I will, of course, take the opportunity to encourage positive thinking and reactions as much as you can and as often as you can.

Back to the self-cross-examination. Why do you think you are ready for a relationship, especially considering how you feel about your past relationships? Meaning, do you actively intend to be better in each relationship? And if so, what is your definition of better? Having specific goals and ambitions for your life is important and helps form the driving force of your actions and pursuits thereafter. Similarly, if you do have the ambition of one day being married, then you must work just as actively and consistently on this goal as any other. With this approach, though you understand the weight of the ambition, you also appreciate why I am cautioning you not to rush or completely rule out your intuition. It is all about balance.

And again, if you are to accept relationship advice from others outside this relationship, while I understand you may automatically cleave to your peers, I implore you to balance that with advice from someone trusted and more mature by virtue of experience honed over more years than you have. If you are unable to convince such a person of your relationship readiness, it means you need more work. At least this way, you give yourself the opportunity to be fair. Otherwise, accepting advice, solely from someone who has never had a similar experience, is akin to a child giving the parent advice on how to parent.

Ambitious thinkers go after their dreams. For the most part, every person should possess ambition to do something bigger and better. This is no different for relationships. Those involved should seek to acquire success in their relationships too. This doesn't mean chasing marriage as the means of success, certainly not if it means rushing into your relationship. Again, intellect and intuition need to agree.

You may ask your peers to give their opinion on the matter of relationships, but ultimately, it is up to you, with your discernment and level of maturity, to be able to assess the advice you get because quite literally, not all advice will be given with good intentions toward you. You would also have to be able to carefully discern, especially if people perceive that you are vulnerable and thus more gullible. You must balance your instincts with your intellect as a young person, especially as you will seek more often to take advice from your peers.

Conversely, there are some of the young people who act differently from their peers, by virtue of thinking differently. They are more mature than their peers, and they are more grounded in their beliefs and value systems, they are to be recognized.

The preceding advice about discernment is for those young people to whom these reasons apply. As for those young people who are opposite of the ones I just described, it is more that they would settle for anything that is quick and easy. These are the ones who can still be described as caterpillars, with the potential to transform nonetheless. Consider this book one of the leaves in that bottle.

The single most important thing that propelled me into my relationship, which to me is a success, is my Christian belief, my belief in Jesus Christ, the Son of God. Prior to my found religion, I partook in ungodly and immoral practices too.

Years ago, when I was compelled to say, "I do," my belief in God played a large role. Prior to my conversion and accepting the grace of God, one could call me a double agent. I led two lives. I would party all night and be at church the next morning, participating in Communion on occasion, dating several women at a time, which would also require lying. I did it all. Hallelujah for saving grace!

When I was in school as a youth, I remember in science class, we did a project on butterflies—the transformation of a caterpillar into a butterfly rather. We would place this caterpillar in a bottle of leaves and over the course of days, watch natural transformation take place. It would help to contextualize transformation in this way. Each stage of our life is an opportunity to transform into better versions of ourselves and ultimately produce better relationships.

I am thankful for the power of transformation, which starts in the small way and works its way up to more urgent sentiments. Since we all will transform, it is inevitable, whether we like it or not, for the good or the bad; I therefore implore you to pay attention and remain present in your mind. Do not try to go against transformation, especially if you believe it poses a threat to your current lifestyle. That too can transform; it's just like that science project of watching a caterpillar transform into a butterfly. You must truthfully assess where you are on the transformation spectrum and, even more so, what makes you think you can achieve what you set out to at this time, based on where you are. I can ask the questions; only you can answer them.

In 1 John 4:1 (NKJV), the Bible gives us some guidelines and instructions regarding discernment. As a believer, I pull for this scripture to discern spirits, and I am reassured by "Beloved, do not believe every spirit, but test the spirits, whether they are of God; because many false prophets have gone into the world." Not only does John say to be aware of the spirits but also to test them, so that you are not deceived. And for my readers who are believers of the faith, I take it a step further to be so cautious as to avoid deception. When skillfully and tactfully done, deception will not resemble deception, not until it is too late to guard against it and the havoc it will create. I say to believers to cleave to like-minded believers for certain advice, but even then, be discerning.

Both my wife and I can share personal accounts on this subject, because when I announced my plans to get married, even believers in my inner circle cautioned against me going through with it, on account of the information they had, notwithstanding me informing them of the divine intervention that had led me to my wife. Had I listened, I would have lost out on thirty-three years of love, for starters. My wife too can share that she had to trust her own instincts and her own faith. If not, we would not be together. I am thankful that we both did not listen solely to those voices.

For both of us, it was essential that we acknowledge God as the owner of the institution of marriage and allow our spirituality to thrive within the marriage; we avoided any pitfalls this way. Sadly, I have observed the opposite in other relationships, some of which were also expressed in counseling.

My wife and I are thankful every day that we did not listen to naysayers but instead to His voice in our hearts because "His voice makes the difference and when He speaks, He relieves our troubled minds." Believer or no believer, there is little to no contest that marriage was made by God; hence any amount of preparation for the same should in some way involve Him—not just for convenience and societal benefits but as a conscious inclusion by yourself and your partner to acknowledge the authority of marriage.

The moment you begin to see your own self transform, as you ponder the responsibilities and weight of marriage and look forward to it with open arms, is a sign for the go-ahead. You are ready. Are you there yet? What evidence do you have to present to yourself toward that claim?

What that means is that you will slowly transition from single-doom behavior into a lifestyle that invites responsibility and loyalty. You work on your ambitions and goals, and while you continuously work on yourself to be better versions of yourself each day, you also work on discerning your prospects.

For instance, when I have the privilege to engage young men, I always impress upon them the importance of having some form of self-sustenance, where it pertains to having more independence, which cannot be had without financial liberation.

This is reality. You must have some legal and ethical means with which to ply your trade or talent and use that as a means for either money or barter. Self-sufficiency is very important in a relationship. These skills also come in handy to make your household more self-sufficient. This is the reality that you need to appreciate when considering saying, "I do." You need to be able to take care of yourself and your spouse and, as the relationship progresses, your family. Your assessment of self needs to be balanced, as opposed to relying solely on emotions, which are not constant and are prone to being situation-based.

You are also reminded in questioning yourself to also give credence to your inner voice. Spirituality aside, 95 percent of your brain's activity happens on the subconscious level, as information from all your senses is deposited, versus the 5 percent that is conscious. You have the information available, but you must sift for it. Allow yourself the time to look for the patterns of information that you seek, and you should most certainly find it. Do not doubt for a moment that this feeling based on subconscious intelligence is not enough to assist you in your deliberations.

So, tell me again why you think you are ready?

5. WHAT DO I WANT FROM A RELATIONSHIP?

Everyone considering a relationship typically wants the best outcome from the union. Realistically though, all agreements should be entered with no regrets or stipulations. A prenup, for example, which is a written contract, is usually signed to protect the interests of both parties should the relationship take a nosedive.

I respect that everyone has his or her own perspective on the matter, but for me and my wife, we have agreed that a prenup would do more harm than good, especially when entering such a union as marriage, which should be "till death do us part." Mark 10:7–9 (NKJV) substantiates the cohesiveness of marriage and declares that for this reason, a man shall leave his father and mother. It exemplifies how a man leaves his parents to be joined to his wife, and the two become one—in other words, glued together.

Using the practical context of "yoke," we can understand how God intended marriages to be. Being yoked in marriage is likened to two oxen being yoked together by their necks to carry out tasks. A yoke is a wooden item that links the two oxen together through a harness. There is no separation of the two oxen in carrying out their tasks, such as plowing the field, while they are yoked. They function together, and where one goes, so does the other. This is how God's word describes marriage to be.

The writer of the scripture in Mark 10:9 (NKJV) stated, "Therefore what God has joined together, let not man separate." This also is crucial for a believer; hence it is even more important to know if a union is a man-joined or God-joined marriage. It is essential to know what type of relationship you want and what you want from it. It is crucial to remain cognizant that the appeal for marriage stems from different reasons; some marry because of immigration, to preserve a family legacy, to substantiate a pregnancy, for sex and money, and the list goes on. Some marry even hoping marriage would transform a person.

You must know what kind of marriage you want, so you know what kind of marriage to avoid. Of course, if you hope for your relationship to culminate in marriage, then it is advisable that your relationship be founded on strong and durable precepts, including love; otherwise, your relationship would be more vulnerable. In other words, marriage should not be taken lightly. How long exactly do you expect this relationship to last?

Take a building, for example. As a contractor by profession, I have witnessed the demise of great and small buildings alike on account of a weak foundation, which I alluded to earlier. All the buildings looked grand and appeared to be of solid foundation when, in fact, that was not the case, and they crumbled at the slightest turbulence in the earth. What type of foundation do you want for your relationship?

It is such a sad eye-opener how important the foundation really is— and not just what seems to be the case. I recall esteeming certain couples to a certain degree as I sought to emulate their relationship goals only to find out about their divorce years later. While I wanted to emulate them, I am indeed happy that a common denominator in my wife's and my marriage is believing in God and His will being the sustenance of our marriage. These are some of the points to consider when you assess that realistically you have deemed yourself ready for a relationship. Now you must break down some of the things you want from this relationship. I offer some staples.

1. Appreciation is the recognition or admiration from someone you hold in high esteem. In this case, your spouse would be one such person. It is not unnatural to want attention from your spouse, but how much attention do you need? And how much attention is classified as healthy and meeting the needs of both partners? Moreover, what will you do if you do not get that attention?

Appreciation can manifest itself in many ways, and even the seemingly insignificant actions can be a love language for you and your partner, as they show him or her that you consider his or her feelings. Helping with the chores, observing your spouse's birthday, and so on are all ways you can communicate appreciation through the thought you put into the action. We learn from each other, and we take turns, so that each partner can get relief sometimes. Your spouse will notice. He or she will see that you wish him or her relief and will feel appreciated. You can also never go wrong by telling your partner how much you appreciate him or her. It boosts his or her morale and that of the relationship.

Another way I show my appreciation is by treating my wife completely on her birthday, spoiling her, if you will. She does the same for me when it is my birthday. We treat each other when it is our anniversary, and we are not shy of vacationing outside the United States on these special occasions. What remains constant is that we do this to show each other that we value and appreciate each other.

Special occasions aside, another way to show appreciation is by sharing in the chores. I give my wife a break sometimes and completely takes over the chores without her having to ask. I have my mom to thank for encouraging me when I paid attention while she was in the kitchen. This made me into a man who wouldn't have to wait until my wife was keeling over from exhaustion to help. Moreover, there is a sense of enjoyment in simply doing something, anything, for my spouse.

2. Honesty is speaking the truth, even after doing something wrong—especially then. Honesty goes hand in hand with building trust and engendering openness in your relationship. Your partner deserves to be able to trust your honesty, regardless of what he or she wants to hear. If you don't feel like sharing a detail, it is better you admit so than lie; the aim is to always be as open and honest as possible. It builds confidence in your relationship, and confidence boosts effort. Confidence gives your relationship a greater fighting chance regardless of how uncomfortable or controversial the subject of the discussion may become. To encourage honesty and being open in the relationship, nonjudgmental communication must be an active practice in your relationship, as it helps both parties to develop consistency to present the fact.

You or your partner may not be inclined to open up if you have a fear of being judged and not only being judged but being treated differently after being judged. Try not to come to premature conclusions about what your partner is trying to say and understand that he or she may trust you with information not readily shared otherwise.

Not actively investing in engendering a culture of honesty in your relationship will directly and indirectly allow dishonesty to take root. This will contribute to hostile, sometimes toxic, all-round unhealthy behaviors in the relationship, especially when there is no intent to remedy the situation. There should not be a culture of lying for any reason, as the contempt from this practice will be allowed to fester to the point where the damages may be irreparable.

3. Sharing life experiences—being in a relationship means you have someone whom you look forward to sharing tales from your life with. That is a two-way street, equally trodden. Sharing portions of your history, in healthy doses, with each

other allows the partners to understand and better appreciate how important certain values and ideals are to each other. It can also make them an advocate for each other. This way, your partner will find it easier to support you in any way possible, depending on the opportunities or challenges that may arise in your relationship. In essence, if you do feel that getting bored in your relationship is normal, then probably more sharing needs to take place. It is like helping your partner unpack his or her baggage but also discovering any hidden treasures he or she may have locked away. It is an adventure; treat your relationship like an adventure.

Seeing your relationship as an adventure would mean that there is less feeling bored as a couple. When I hear about couples being bored, I despair. Surely someone can strike up an enjoyable conversation or an activity that both people would enjoy. There should be so many opportunities for fun, even if it is just to reminisce. Sharing life experiences is like unlocking wisdom. It is a journey of discovery for you and your partner. My wife and I take a leisurely and laugh-filled stroll down memory lane all the time. Sometimes, we recall our first impressions of each other, down to the tiniest detail, like how we were dressed.

We recall just learning certain things about each other, seeing as we had different cultural experiences in some respects, and it was like creating history, our history. We recounted friendships and family practices—again, the emphasis on a belly full of laughter. There were sobering moments, each with its own lessons that we tried to glean after healing from the pain, but thank God, we could always look back and have a laugh. We both started the parenting journey together, and so we have that shared bond. It worked because we drew from our different upbringings when it came to raising our first child, and the differences are sometimes obvious. It is whatever you and your partner can bond over.

Sharing relies on communication, so one can even say sharing strengthens communication skills within a relationship—at least it has been so for my wife and me. Without communication, there would be no relationship, and once we communicate by sharing our life experiences, we learn the importance of valuing what each partner brings to the relationship. We are not shy communicators, and both agree that especially in relationships, there is some amount of melding of souls that needs to take place, as it holds the relationship together.

4. Transparency in a relationship is akin to honesty but with more emphasis on the emotional side of you. This allows your partner to see beneath the history and many roles you may play, to who you are at the core. This includes opening up about your vulnerabilities, fears, and dreams alike, that you wouldn't dream of sharing with just anyone.

Transparency means to put down your guards, unveil your masks, and remove all clutter that can hinder your vision. Transparency means to put your hands up and surrender to each other.

In Ephesians 5:21 (NKJV), we read, "Submitting to one and other in the fear of God." Paul was speaking to the church. When he addressed husbands and wives, he declared they were to submit to one another. In this context, both parties were equally called to submit, as opposed to just wives submitting to their husbands.

Submission is the highest form of humility and obedience and is no respecter of financial status, societal status, and so on. It is merely your readiness to be available for your partner. Without this humility, transparency may even be more difficult. How important is humility in your relationship? Ironically, the more mature a person is, the easier it is for him or her to be humble, because that is the whole point. So yes, be prepared to help your partners to chase his or her dreams, while he or she supports your ambitions as well, but ambitions aside, there should be a unanimous agreement to always submit to each other, in any given moment.

Transparency in a relationship should begin from the very inception and become more practiced as the relationship progresses. Even if you are not asked for the information, it is recommended that you share as much information as possible. For instance, sharing your intent to do something but without all the details is not transparent.

Transparency in marriage means each partner commits to or agrees to open, honest interaction. Transparency is not when partners hide information from each other because they feel as though it will mitigate arguments. I pull for statistics to prove that more transparency equals fewer arguments in your relationship and contributes to its longevity. Not being transparent prevents valuable information from being shared, information that potentially could have prevented some arguments or disagreements. A simple example would be sharing with your spouse that you purchased something for a friend but neglecting to mention that that friend is male or female. You can see how a much later revelation may raise many questions for your spouse.

There are also two areas where being as honest as possible, as soon as possible, is most important. Those are your health and your wealth. In 3 John 3:2 (NKJV), we read, "Beloved, I wish above all things that thou mayest prosper, and be in health, even as thy soul prospered." Apostle John declared this to Gaius.

In this way, emphasis on health, especially being transparent about your health, can lead to fewer problems. Let's say something does happen, resulting in a health scare; you sharing that information, would put less strain on your partner. Typically, households are less encouraging of men sharing their health statuses. This practice has led to many marriages prematurely dissolving when the husbands have fallen ill beyond recovery. Wives become widows too early and all due to not knowing their partners had a condition. Even when they do find out, it is too late.

Take for instance, me feeling unwell and contracting the flu—because of my own negligence, I'll admit. Instead of warning my wife, soon, it became obvious that I was sick because of my symptoms, which my wife had to witness.

Moving on from health to wealth, I mentioned in the beginning my disagreement with prenuptial agreements, as they always seem to be that lack of reconciliation in the event of a disagreement, because at that time in the relationship, all that goes through the minds of each partner is the gains from the relationship, despite its demise. In fact, the apostle said his prayer was for all of us to prosper. In the matter of finances and material gains, transparency is even less often practiced. One can see where a prenup is predisposed to offer couples a way out of a relationship, allowing them to give up prematurely on a relationship but still manage to come away with financial gains, which they may feel is their due. I hope that is clear.

I hasten to say not all relationships end in divorce or separation, but a lack of transparency accounts for quite a number of those separations. Transparency in finances in your marriage is important, and you must consider what you want for your own relationship where it pertains to finances. For instance, how do you intend to handle transparency wherein you may make more than your partner and vice versa? The Bible is the fundamental guideline for transparency. Ephesians 4:25 (NKJV) says, "Therefore putting away lying. Let each of you speak the truth with his neighbor, for we are members with one another."

The operative word here is *lying*, wherein Paul warns against lying among believers, a relationship problem that exists in the church. Even more so, in the relationship between yourself and your partner, lying should be even further avoided. There is an old saying, "Speak the truth and speak it ever'cause it what it will. He who hides the wrong he did, will do the wrong thing still."

It is a slippery slope to always remain transparent. One lie, just one, is all that is needed to rock an otherwise solid relationship. It tends to be more prevalent on the topic of money. What type of stance would you like your relationship to have on money? Would you be open to joint accounts? Would you be content with knowing as little as possible about your partner's money, because he or she worked for it and you want him or her to regard yours with as much privacy? Because you or your partner earned it? Remember, finance is important.

5. Intimacy—what is intimacy in a marriage? Intimacy is the closeness of your relationships in various ways: spiritually, emotionally, intellectually, sexually, financially, and socially, among others. Intimacy should never be an end to a great moment, but rather a journey that lasts through your marriage. Intimacy is deepened with friendship and is an important bonding agent for couples. If there is no intimacy in your relationship, I recommend counseling.

I have a few beginners' tips on establishing intimacy in your relationship, as once people hear about intimacy, they immediately think that it culminates in sex or is solely about sex. Intimacy is a chance to bond; it is more than just hugging and kissing. It is also about enjoying the closeness of each other's company. Intimacy includes doing fun things that both people enjoy while strengthening the bond in the relationship. It gives both parties the opportunity to be affectionate and caring toward each other, displaying outwardly what they feel on the inside toward their partner. It is be able to laugh with your partner, having inside jokes, and appreciating both the small things and the grand.

It does take some amount of patience to get to a comfortable place where it is easier to be affectionate and intimate with your partner, without always culminating in sex; however, at the same time, you must consider your partner's body like a treasure and invest in discovering all about your partner. All this discovery is time-consuming and would go a long way in maintaining a healthy dose of intimacy in the relationship. Physical intimacy should not be forced. If, for some reason, either partner is aggressive, especially in the bedroom, this should be discussed in a safe space for both parties, so that this can be avoided in the future. Partners should be open-minded to setting boundaries and limits in the relationship to mitigate similar pitfalls.

Again, you would have been engendering a space of openness and nonjudgment, and all this will help your partner to feel relaxed and accepted around you. Intimacy also requires a healthy dose of attention to your partner, the kind that shows him or her that while you actively chase your ambitions with him or her supporting you, there is a "we" time that is uncompromised, and you remain committed to having that "we" time. This means everything should have its time, and unless there is some emergency, there should be balance. When it is electronics time—TV, phones, tablets, and so on—that should not go over into "couple time." If left uncontrolled, these activities could serve more as a distraction and possible detriment to your relationship than anything else.

The point of intimacy is human connection, so again, a healthy dose of intimacy should be accomplished while paying attention to your devices, each in its own time.

I explore intimacy up to the point of sex, which also is equally important. Matthew 19:6 (a) (NKJV) says, "So then, they are no longer two but one flesh." For believers, it is important that we agree that God created sex to be enjoyed between two married people, and sex outside of marriage will be judged by God, as sex is used outside of His intentions. Hebrews 13:4 (NKJV) declares that "Marriage is honorable among all, and the bed undefiled, but fornicators and adulterers God will judge."

Additionally, the word of God says that marriage is honorable, meaning it speaks respect and high regard. Because it is easier for believers to be guided by the word of God, it is that much more difficult for nonbelievers to appreciate the sanctity of marriage and the ramifications of infidelity. One's sexual explorations should remain within the relationship once it is an exclusive relationship. The quality of your relationship will be impacted by the sexual aspect. What kind of sexual lifestyle and practice do you foresee for your relationship? If your relationship does culminate in marriage, how do you mitigate the inevitable temptations of sexual immorality wherein one partner contemplates infidelity?

In 1 Corinthians 7:5 (NKJV), the Bible declares, "Do not deprive one another except with consent for a time that you may give yourself to fasting and prayer and come together so that Satan does not tempt you because of your lack of self-control." Any sex outside these boundaries is a sin. The bodies of a husband and wife belong to each other. The husband should fulfill his marital duty to his wife, and his wife should do the same. Unfortunately, the foregoing statement has eroded the minds of a wide cross-section of husbands and wives, simply because modern relationships do not embrace what the word of God commands in intimacy. This is the reason infidelity is so prevalent in our society.

6. Love—every successful marriage should be built on the foundation of love. Love is the main ingredient that binds husband and wife together. I purposefully built up to love, to emphasize that love doesn't exist in a vacuum or on its own, nor does it appear magically. All of this is intertwined in love, and understandably should be a staple in a husband-and-wife relationship. The Bible exhorts that there is no fear in love, but perfect love drives out fear, because fear torments. Authentic love would meet the needs of both partners, encourage intimacy, and build a lifelong friendship.

The fact that it is one of my later topics in no way means it is less important, and I share some of the ways in which my wife and I work on our love language overtime. Expressing love for one another gives both parties a sense of belonging. Again, love is not just one single action but all the actions combined. That provides something meaningful to you and your partner and, by extension, your relationship. They are as follows:

A. My wife and I like to take leisurely strolls as part of our "we" time. It provides us with quality time away from the responsibilities of the world and our children, and we get to focus solely on us.
B. My wife and I try to work with facts often, as much as we can get them. We try not to jump to conclusions and to be patient with each other.

C. Disputes and misunderstandings, despite our best efforts, are sometimes unavoidable. We try to focus on the root of the problem and find a solution. Once we have, we work on forgiving each other.
D. We take showers together; we use the time also as "we" time, and this is also an opportunity to explore each other.
E. We play games together, simply because we appreciate the opportunity to laugh with each other. If you want to add flair to your relationship, try adding intimate incentives to your games.
F. We plan a meal together, from start to finish, and get creative in the kitchen while we are at it. My wife and I, being from different nationalities, added the variety to our recipe times, and we try to do this at least twice a month. We create something together, even if it is completely unknown to us—after trying our own nation's dishes, that is.
G. We travel together. My wife and I traveled to Dubai, and we got the opportunity to experience a new and diverse culture together. We looked back on our time in Dubai as part of our love language, as we both learned new things about each other on that trip. It was a wow experience.
H. Take your partner to the spa to improve your circulation, relieve muscle tension, and increase mobility, especially if your partner does not like the gym. There are different types of massages to stimulate the entire body: facial, head, and full-body massages. In addition, there are manicures and pedicures that you can experience with your partner, for the pleasing aesthetic and boosting of the spirit. For example, my wife gifted me with a trip to the Royalton in Grenada for my birthday (yes, I am writing from the poolside). It goes without saying that we have been having a wonderful time.

7. We have openness in our marriage. This requires sincerity and honesty because once you say, "I do," I sincerely encourage that you consciously decide to put away games. The bottom line is unhealthy and incriminating secrets are not solid foundations of longstanding relationships. This applies to secrets you had before you got married and during your marriage. You must work with the assumption that these secrets will be found out, which typically they will, sooner or later, and it would be a lot more reassuring if your spouse has already heard about them from you.

Pulling from personal experience, men whom I held as close associates were all witnessed having affairs to the demise of their marriages, sometimes due to their spouses not just finding out but more so them being caught in the act. Openness is crucial. If you are reticent about opening up, it means whatever secret is held over your relationship has the power to shatter its foundation, especially when that secret is held over the relationship, and then that secret is shared outside of your relationship.

Don't assume that your secret is unforgivable; you are arriving at conclusions without giving your spouse the benefit of the doubt. What your spouse may find more unforgiveable is your lack of trust to involve him or her secretly sooner. Love has the power to forgive, and if you love, you must believe in its capabilities.

8. We maintain healthy boundaries. Boundaries protect husbands and wives as individuals. Boundaries can be healthy, and are crucial for maintaining individuality within the partners, while serving the relationship. Both parties should discuss these boundaries until they reach agreement. It is better that both parties are aware of the boundaries and have the same concept of privacy in the relationship, as opposed to each party having a different concept that he or she is working with.

If you and your partner, in contrast, believe there is no such thing as boundaries or privacy in the relationship, if it works, then it is up to you. The bottom line is if you are introducing a concept to the relationship, both parties should be aware and in agreement.

If you and your partner are considering boundaries in the relationship, you are advised to have that conversation before saying, "I do." It can be about the seemingly simple things like "me" time, guilty pleasures, recreational habits, and so on. Once it exists, I recommend you speak to your spouse. If you find there is no mutually satisfying agreement being arrived at, then I recommend again to see a Christian counselor.

9. We practice acceptance in marriage. This is when both parties have expressed unwavering commitment to each other as they are. In the scope of wider society, this is the root of many social ills, so I concede that it may not be so easy. Acceptance is not only being comfortable with someone's faults but also accepting your spouse's diversity and ambitions. If your relationship has healthy boundaries from the outset, that should make acceptance that much easier.

After saying "I do," you can then nurture acceptance, so both parties can thrive and thus the relationship can also thrive. There is no other way to say it: acceptance of the healthy kind is an absolute must in any relationship that wants to go somewhere. Acceptance is one of the keys for a happy marriage; it is the most absolute necessity of all marriage rules. It is also cautioned that pretending to accept is not encouraged, because always, your true intentions will be revealed.

In summary, the preceding are to be deliberated on, and I strongly encourage that you classify them as staples when you ask yourself the question of what you want from your relationship.

The entirety of this publication is meant to be your guide in a strong and promising direction, but all the choices are ultimately up to you and your partner.

6. WHAT DO I HAVE TO OFFER IN A RELATIONSHIP?

I will just jump into it; it is reckless to enter a relationship without clear expectations, what you want and, more so, what you are prepared to give. If what the relationship needs to thrive you are not prepared to give, then that admittance is also okay if you are honest from early on.

Because marriage consists of a man and a woman, both partners need to enter the marriage with individual perspectives as it relates to each's contribution to the relationship prior to saying I do. What each person contributes to the relationship should be addressed preferably during courtship or even engagement, any step prior to marriage. Prevention is better than getting into a relationship when you know you are not quite ready and will instead be spending countless hours correcting errors. That is not wisdom.

Entering an intimate relationship is like constructing a building. You will need the right types of professionals and the materials to construct this building. First, you cannot construct a building if you do not have a blueprint (architectural drawings) to guide you. The blueprints would then determine the scope and size of the potential building. It is coupled with the professionals trained to work with what is presented. A partner's contribution is no different. When you know what you are working with, it brings a sense of direction, peace, and comfort between partners.

Prior to my wife and I saying, "I do," we were engaged in several conversations relating to our individual contributions and the direction of the relationship. One of the lessons we learned is that we were able to identify the type of character we were about to be married to. It made us excited to tie the knot. There are two parts to this process, as I have come to realize: premarital and post marital. We say a lot of good things and make promises in the beginning. But when we get into the reality of the relationship, we are unable to maneuver the challenges. Fortunately, my wife and I were able to maintain the expectation of each other and exceed those expectations on occasions.

It is reckless to just land yourself in a relationship. It will not last unless you plan for your future. This is the only way to add value to a hopeful long-term relationship. You must consider your likes, dislikes, passions, skills, personality, honesty, limitations, and the list go on. It is also reckless not to spend the quality time to think about some of the plans you make together. Excitement is good, but again, balance is key. In this case, it would be another dose of reality and practicality.

1. Sense of family values—I take the opportunity to impress upon you that the family unit is the first form of society and thus creates the very fabric of the wider human society. The foundation of society, if you may, is families first and then communities and everything in between. The families are the manufacturing grounds for the members of society in a few years, and depending on the values expressed in any family, the contribution to society will be desired or undesired. The practice of the families, the first social unit, and their values are what are reenacted when the younger generations grow up—from religious beliefs to ideals and other social practices.

There is every possibility it is all being passed down from one generation to another—again, whether good or bad, socially acceptable or not, moral or immoral.

How do you feel about your family or the concept of family? And what values from your own family do you intend to adopt in your relationship? The healthy way of families is not dissimilar to the practices encouraged in relationships, but by the mere result of society, it is clear such practices were woefully lacking and will continue to be lacking until each family realizes the power of being better at being a family and creating better societies. Families should be a safe place for members to come and share their ideas about life, where there is acceptance and not shunning of members. It is just like a relationship.

It is essential that partners share a similar view on family matters. In this way, compatibility must be present. It starts with the simple things. Let's say you marry a German man, whose only language is German, and you only speak fluent Spanish; there will be no communication taking place on account of language barriers. Similar values will ensure that you will be better able to navigate life and its challenges together. Even with the best communication, if there is no shared value system in the relationship, then it will not be enough.

What do I mean by family? Traditionally, a mother, a father, and their children. Value is what is valued or treasured. This means ideas, beliefs, and practices passed down from generation to generation. It is important with whom you choose to carry on this tradition. Other traditional values include anniversaries, birthdays, vacationing and other special occasions, and, of course, religion, which is a very strong tradition in a lot of households.

Of course, we would all have to agree on what the concept of a healthy family looks like, but that's for another book. I am all for diversity, but you must weigh the pros and cons when marrying outside your shared social experience and determine how to navigate the differences. It is always advisable to marry someone who has similar beliefs or interests. In this case, communication is even more important.

2. Patience and tolerance go hand in hand and work best both ways. Anything can test one's patience, no matter how in love or humble one is. It is the response to this test, however, that is crucial and mitigates further tests. You must ascertain the magnitude of the test, possibly deduce why it tests your partner's patience, and work from there. In essence, how does this test compare to the grander scheme of things?

Case in point, I have been happily married for thirty-three years now (yes, my wife and I are proud of us), but there is no absence of tests in our relationship. For instance, my wife usually comments on my loud prayers. I have a habitual praying schedule, and sometimes, without my meaning to, my passion increases my volume while I am praying, depending on the subject. It happens especially when I am praying for all and sundry. I beg my wife for patience and tolerance during these times, but sometimes that tolerance feels like it has been stretched.

Patience and tolerance also manifest themselves in the mere absence of angry outbursts and so on, without consciously trying to be patient or tolerant.

Tolerance is most evident in our displays of restraint, especially in the face of conflicts, disagreements, and clear contests to our core as human beings. Each such encounter, however, should increasingly portray the importance of tolerance. Peace cannot be achieved otherwise, and peace in your relationship is a staple, as your relationship may not thrive without it. Would you honestly say that these values are important in your relationship, and are you prepared to display them?

Patience is no doubt a stabilizer for relationships, manifesting as endurance in some. Patience is never in vain and can never be enough. Within patience lies the trait of self-restraint and being slow to act out of anger. For believers, patience is a virtue, and it is a sure teacher of patience. One teacher of patience is the challenges that press you to work them through, and the more you respond in anger, the longer it takes to learn and move on from that challenge. It is important to view any perceived challenge that your relationship faces as a lesson in patience. There is no way around the teacher of patience and tolerance.

Patience is a virtue for believers; it is akin to emotional intelligence for nonbelievers. The principle is pretty much the same, and it is especially required in direct conflicts and disagreements in your relationship. I recommend you not recklessly provoke your partner, if at all, but at least have an open discussion about disputes and how to handle them in the relationship from its neophyte stages.

Because humans are made up of emotions, it would take tolerance to stabilize or balance the way we conduct ourselves during conflicts and disagreements. Tolerance acts as an antidote to normalize unusual behavior in your relationship. Like patience, tolerance is gained through trials and tribulations. Again, once evident, please address certain concerns before tying the knot. Personality will be a big part of how some of these conversations play out. You need to discuss how to handle spontaneous outbursts ahead of time.

3. Dependability, reliability, and responsibility are other staples for a relationship of substance and ones that can withstand time. I will caution that these traits, technically all of them, are best marked by actions and not necessarily vague words. These traits are also not easily explained away by excuses for not coming through, so be vigilant.

   A. Dependability is a cornerstone not just of your relationship but the quality of trust within the relationship. This means your spouse can depend on your word. Your word should be your bond, because it is usually followed by action. About promises, again I say, it is healthy to fantasize, but a dose of reality is usually required to balance one's expectations. It doesn't have to start heavy right away but with the little minute details in a day that some may dismiss as inconsequential: being on time, following through if one makes a pledge to do so, and the like; then you can move on to more impactful occasions, where lack of dependability reflects poorly not just on the character of your spouse but on you as well. Another point to note is only to observe your spouse's dependability within your relationship but also outside of the relationship.

Ironically, I am writing amid the global health pandemic of COVID-19, which will not slow down if those we delegate the power to act do not do so in the ways we expect them to. Unless there is a change, the current trajectory will worsen. All positions of power, from the president to the governors to all the mayors and ultimately the citizens should realize their responsibility and act together to deflate the impact of COVID-19. Objectively, we all have a responsibility to rely and depend on one another, to stop the spread of COVID-19, which results in death. It is no different in a relationship. There is nothing more painful than depending on your partner to act responsibly on a critical matter only to be let down.

    B. Reliability—right now, I continue to write this book. It is March 30, 2020. The race for reliability continues around the clock, as we all rely on each other to do our part as authorities ask, to prevent the spread of COVD-19. Successful relationships must be adaptable, based on the subject, but ultimately should be relied upon. It cannot be that you leave your partner to hang on to your bare words with no actions or fulfilment of those words. Understandably, your partner will not do this for long, especially when he or she realized he or she cannot rely on you. Men mostly usually "miss the water when the well runs dry."

A reliable partner finishes what he or she starts, no matter how long it takes. Reliable partners are focused, because they know their partner is depending on them. Reliable partners are not double-minded. James 1:8 (NKJV) declares that a "double-minded man is unstable in all of his ways." Unstable relationships do not endure. Instability, however, can be recognized in the early stages of dating. Avoid the mistake of thinking that marriage will solve all your problems overnight.

Reliable partners do not overpromise because they are aware that humans fail sometimes. They are aware that relationships will experience some disappointments. They instead try to adopt an approach that manages the expectations in the relationship. Sometimes, these expectations are unrealistic from the beginning, but it still incites a feeling of dissatisfaction if not met. As a partner, do not make promises to fulfill unrealistic requests. Reliability calls for teamwork, and as a couple, you both play to win. To win, it means discipline, which goes hand in hand with reliability, and you have a more satisfactory relationship.

Couples who are focused on being reliable to each other develop a consistent rhythm. They also embrace a sense of service, which in my opinion is the highest act of humility and again is crucial for relationships, meaning, if you are not humble, you will not serve your partner fully, much less find pleasure in doing so. A reliable couple shares the burdens. Each shoulders the whole burden of his or her partner if needs be. It is not uncommon, nowadays, for the man and woman to be able to identify their roles and responsibilities, and it is not a bad step; it means each partner can be relied upon to fulfill these roles once he or she is able, with consistency.

>   C. Responsibility is where we end up. It is that state of accountability, being held accountable for your promises and pledges. It is healthy in a relationship to hold each other accountable, not just for couple goals but also individual goals. Accountable means answerable for actions or decisions. Accountability is not a blame game but more a learning curve for each partner. Accountability is not a stick with which to whip a partner and highlight shortcomings. It is more like a compassionate conversation on improvement once your partner expresses the desire for your accountability approach. Are you prepared to be held accountable and to hold your partner accountable? Responsibility demands

patience, understanding, humility, and impartiality to charter any relationship in an amicable manner.

With the absence of responsibility comes poor management. This has caused many organizations to fail, and it will no doubt have the same effect on your relationship. Failure is bred when there is a lack of maturity, which takes the form in the willingness of one to tolerate his or her partner and his or her shortcomings.

I take every opportunity to talk to youth because the concept of responsibility is never discussed too much. I give them advice on their education, career, family planning, you name it. Most of the time, there is a sense of nonchalance in their responses; however, I am not discouraged by this. I recall my youthful years spent a little differently. I was no stranger to the concept of responsibility, and it never left me. Because it never did, I was always prepared or at least taking steps to be prepared.

Responsibility will be required of both partners, as the transition from singlehood to ultimately marriage will require attention, focus, and a sense of purpose. Imagine investing a million dollars and it fails. It will have long-lasting impacts on you; a relationship and such investments are no different.

An accountability check in any setting requires maturity and kindness, hence the importance of maturity. It is not something that can be downloaded; one must be sincere in the transformation of one's mind. Do not be discouraged if your attempts at accountability checking are met with reticence for whatever reason. You proceed, as you are invested. And, of course, this not only applies to intimate relationships. Self-accountability always helps a process, but then you must be able to a certain extent to support a relationship while that is being honed in you or your partner. Business organizations are like relationships, since imperfect people are involved in the equation. Build on this.

Once you have committed to each other, there must be a foundation of trust on which you build. Trust must be accorded to each partner simply because. This trust should be able to withstand temptations, which are sure to come. This will prepare you for *collective responsibility*, which is where collaboration is at its highest. This does not mean that you commit an actual crime with your partner, but you should be responsible for each other.

It helps the sanity of the relationship also if, as a couple, you both agree to not be swayed by external opinions and voices. Decisions should be made solely within the relationship, even if there is advice allowed from outside. This sets a healthy boundary for the relationship for the future. Remember that you are now one flesh instead of two. As Matthew 19:6 (NKJV) says, "What therefore God hath joined together, let no man put asunder."

Do not be intimidated by responsibilities in relationships. They will grow with you, and they will also change. Do not fear the inevitability either. For instance, twenty years ago, I had no problem with all the responsibilities I had as a husband, business owner, and minister; fast-forward twenty years, and I am considering giving up some of those things. This means I am responsible enough to admit that my physical abilities are not the same as they were twenty years ago, and I adjust accordingly.

All these checklists are especially important for someone going from single to dating to ultimately being married. Use also as a guide Luke 12:48 (NKJV): "But he who did not know, yet committed things deserving of stripes, shall be beaten with few. For everyone to whom much is given, from him much is required; and to whom much has been committed, of him they will ask the more."

Understandably, responsibility is usually evident in acts of duty, and everything is in considering the magnitude of a fallout, so perspective is also always key. It helps to temper one's response toward one's partner. For example, your partner being late may not have the same ramifications as being an unprepared country in a global health pandemic where lives are already being lost, there is no vaccine in sight, and there are not enough resources to combat it in the meantime. So, yes, both issues are important, but perspective is encouraged. I'm not saying that you should give your partner a free pass because the action does not reach a global magnitude, but again, perspective breeds patience and grows humility, as it becomes a teaching point for your relationship.

Factors to consider in your journey to being more accountable include physical and unavoidable limitations and situations, much like I alluded to above. Limitations may come through physical manifestations, age, health, financial status, and so on. These are just points to consider. What works now may change a few years down the line, based on circumstances getting better or worse. Always be willing to adjust your approaches as a couple and do not be discouraged by constant change.

On many occasions, I have discussed the topic of maturity, and appreciating this trait can help save time and help you in the process of discerning red flags. Off the top of my head, some red flags include public and private embarrassing, name calling and bad-mouthing, habitual lateness, and habitual breaking of promises. These are on the light side, but not surprisingly can be discerned during dating or courting. Again, it may not be directed at you; however, observing these habits is key. There is no maturity residing in these actions.

Now that we have covered the basics in the name of responsibility, I am going to introduce a flip side to this responsibility coin, and that is collective guilt or partners in crime. It only sounds romantic but does not engender healthy relationship practices. What does it look like? Encouraging and supporting poor social ideals, interactions, and behaviors to the point of being culpable for such actions through being complicit. Sounds toxic? It is, to the point of being criminal in some cases. It is not surprising to me though. I have counseled a few people in this situation.

Finally, the best and greatest act of responsibility, especially between a married couple, is to love one another. You are responsible for nourishing the love you pledged to supply throughout your relationship. Ephesians 6:22–23 (NKJV) says, "Whom I have sent to you for this very purpose, that you may know our affairs, and that he may comfort your hearts.

Peace to the brethren, and love with faith, from God the Father and the Lord Jesus Christ."

Apostle Paul admonishes husband and wife to love and submit to one another, and it is as simple as that. Best believe both parties are responsible for enacting this even in the most difficult times and most unsavory of arguments. Within a marriage, it is expected that love abides; it was not meant for haters but for lovers. It means there should be an absence of hate. With that being said, love is strong, love forgives, love is committed, and true love never fails and always comes through. I leave the subject with another admonishment to love like 1 Peter 4:8 (NKJV) says: "And above all things, have fervent love for one another, for love will cover a multitude of sins."

Love is not a distraction or an absentee sport. Love simply dispels all arguments and pains. Are you prepared to hold yourself accountable for loving your partner as you promised, for as long as you promised? Are you prepared to be responsible for your spouse?

4. Respect is just as important as love in a relationship. Respect means acknowledging and recognizing the value of your partner as a human being first and then respecting his or her significance to the success of your marriage. Respect demands equality, and favor is up to the partner but not mandatory. It is the lack of respect in a relationship that will foretell challenges in your relationship if not curtailed as identified. I must emphasize that even though men and women have inherent differences, regardless of personality, temperament, form of expression, and so on, respect must prevail.

Each couple must invest in finding out how best to meet each other halfway—compromise, if need be—but not abandon respect for one minute. If that can be achieved, then the relationship has a chance at being stronger. Remember, the healthier the couple (not just physically), the healthier the relationship. Comfort zones are also a point to consider when discussing the topic of respect, as respect not only covers behaviors and ideals within the context of respect but also in the context of absence of respect, which is just as important. How would you or your spouse react to perceived or blatant disrespect?

When a woman demonstrates disrespect to a man, especially in public, this puts the man in an uncomfortable zone. Women crave affection and attention. There needs to be a balance between these ideals to make a relationship impenetrable. God wired men differently from women, from their personality to their temperament. Women would much more like to talk than a man would offer to strike up a conversation, just as women are more likely to cry and admit their emotions much sooner than a man would. Women are also more emotional and more open in their displays of emotion than a man, and all these must be considered in the conversation about respect, finding a balance between the differences.

Albert Einstein noted, "I speak to everyone the same way, whether the garbage man or the President." In no uncertain terms, Albert Einstein is simply saying that respect should be inherent, regardless of where someone may come from or how he or she may be perceived. The rules are simple: treat everyone with respect and expect respect in return. Even if someone disrespects you, that does not mean you have to disrespect them in return; however, if everyone leads from having respect, then there would be fewer occasions of disrespect.

Within your relationship, pride is the opposite of respect, and so it is even more crucial to try to control pride and how it manifests. Your partner deserves your full respect, and that is always a good place to start. So regardless of your spouse's esteem based on societal evaluations, he or she deserves your full respect.

Discernment will teach you to pick your battles wisely in a relationship, but this should never translate to conditional respect.

Respect is a conscious choice that you must make—the same as with kindness, attitude, and generosity. The manifestations of these, or the lack thereof, are also based on conscious choice to do or not do. Be guided accordingly. You can probe what motivates that choice, but it is not something to be explained away by "I don't know" or the myriad of excuses you'll hear when people refuse to accept responsibility, either for their choices and their consequent actions. All of these are crucial to handling the inevitable challenges and disputes in a relationship. Having a unified outlook on how to handle disputes would also help in this regard. That would guide how your relationship recovers (or not) from its speed bumps.

Respect also is called upon to come to a compromise when your partner broaches the subject of privacy again or if you broach the subject. You must make a lot of decisions as a couple, because it is not only one person anymore, and as a couple, you both decide on how to make these decisions and what factors are to be considered. If there was any time to share weaknesses and proclivities to your partner, it would be in that conversation where you both deliberate on how to make decisions going forward. It may take some trial and error, tears, apologizing with actions, and, for believers, fasting and praying.

Philippians 2:3 (NKJV) declares, "Let nothing be done through selfish ambitions or conceit but in lowliness of mind let each esteem the other better than himself." Paul takes it a step further, driving home the point of humility to believers. Humility is a mark of servanthood, and the Apostle Paul entreats us to be always humble. Service to your partner and humans is not just about putting your needs aside and being subjugated to an ungracious host but more so, gratitude gained from serving your partner and humans. However, it only works if both parties do it. Marriage is all about two imperfect people coming together in an imperfect world.

Hallmarks of this journey and ensuring your success are affirmation, validation, and appreciation. It is crucial to note that whatever you identify to work on in your relationship, once you get the results, you can continue to do this. Not all couples are the same, not by a long shot. It is the little things that matter. Give your spouse a rose, include him or her in your activities, and do not be selfish with your attention.

It not only makes your partner feel good but shows him or her your commitment to the relationship. If you need help with some of these small things, it does not hurt to ask your spouse.

Respect from the beginning begets longevity in a progressive relationship. It will take many forms, all of which are intertwined, such as character, time, patience, attention, truthfulness, and a whole host of other ideals. Respect in relationships is a bedrock of marital satisfaction and happiness.

For believers, we are also reminded that the act of respect is paramount for God our Father. In the courtroom, the highest respect is demanded during sessions; that means nothing but paying attention and adhering to the rules laid out by the court. Conversely, these same rules would apply in church. They are often not adhered to, and instead of complying, some would take it upon themselves to leave the house of God, rather than comply.

Imagine your relationship as the highest court, and there should be fewer issues.

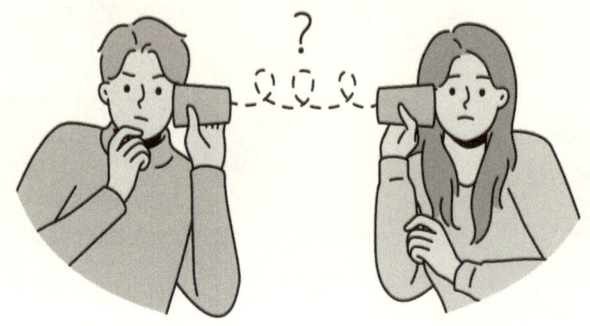

7. EVALUATING YOUR RELATIONSHIP THROUGH THE SWOT ANALYSIS

SWOT is an analysis applied predominantly in the corporate framework where entities evaluate their strengths, weaknesses, opportunities, and threats. SWOT is a simple yet applicable way to evaluate the potential of a relationship. It helps you to budget your time accordingly and know sooner rather than later, the direction of your relationship. Because marriage is a social issue and involves human interaction, misunderstanding is inevitable. SWOT analysis brings to a relationship a simpler way to evaluate and reconcile imperfections in a relationship.

For potential partners who believe that God will send them a partner, I would entreat you to at least consider the possibility of finding that partner, like the Bible says. Proverbs 18:22 (NKJV) gives us a perfect way to phrase it: "He that finds a wife, finds a good thing." Granted, whoever you find more than likely will not be perfect, depending on your definition of perfect anyway.

The SWOT analysis helps you appreciate the practical probabilities of your relationship being successful based on what you use as your grade and what you can tolerate to simplify. The SWOT analysis also helps you to understand and appreciate the interconnectedness of the unsavory details that exist in the relationship along with the positives, to give a balanced picture of how your values can be upheld as you assess your potential partner and, by extension, the relationship. There are no perfect relationships, but because the SWOT analysis is unique and designed to effectuate changes with a holistic approach, I strongly encourage you to explore and apply the SWOT analysis as soon as possible in the relationship, preferably during courtship or dating.

I will explore some pointers on relationship strengths versus weakness, but again, it depends on you and what you want from a relationship. I will also explore opportunities and equally possible threats to mitigate as soon as they are identified.

Use this "SWOT" diagram to navigate your relationship. Focus your efforts in areas that are most urgent then important to you.

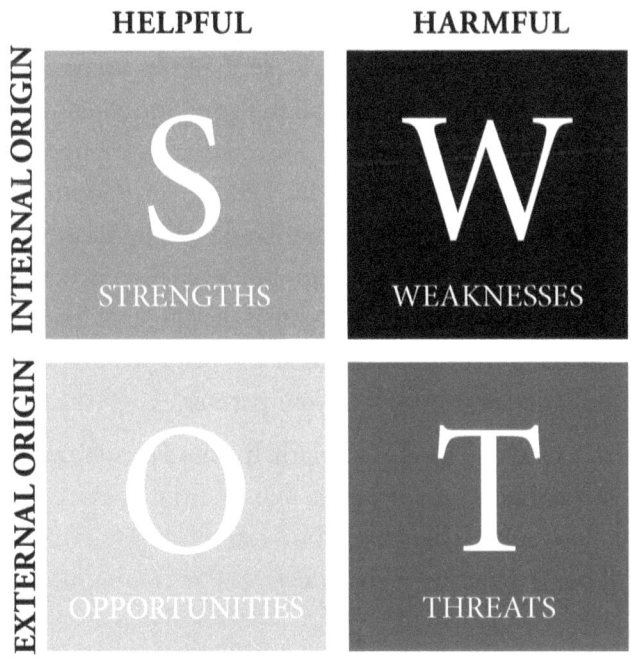

ASSESSING THE STRENGTH OF YOUR RELATIONSHIP

Living in a problem-rich society means that you adapt by being solution-oriented to make the most and experience the fullest in this problem-riddled lifetime. In approaching a relationship and seeing it is a lifetime partnership, both partners must have a firm grasp of their strengths and how these strengths will serve the relationship and each partner. This requires deliberation, as what some may classify as strength may not be perceived as the same by outsiders and, more important, your partner. I'll try to focus on the more obvious strengths. The stronger the individual traits coupled with a commitment to apply them to the relationship, the stronger the relationship could be, with the right applicants. With all that said, if there is no solution, there will be no understanding, and if there is no understanding, there will be no agreement, and the two cannot walk together (Amos 3:3 NKJV).

As you consider your strengths, consider them as those by which you withstand pressure gracefully. For instance, are you a good communicator? If so, why do you think this is so? This cross-examination is important so do not hesitate if you are asked by your partner, which is not unreasonable either.

1. Positive communication is a staple strength, as communication is the medium through which all thoughts are shared, and sharing is also key in every relationship. This communication includes words, body language, and actions in the long run. Communication in all its forms creates a bond and should add immeasurable value to your relationship. Positive communication inspires both partners to understand each other, especially if they are privileged to have eye contact. Positive communication also helps you to share invaluable information and ideas with your partner.

2. Character is also another strength. It is not a person's money, wealth, power, influence, or affluence that determines his or her greatness but his or her character. Your relationship has no foundation without it. I daresay it comes even before communication.

Character is the marrow of reliability; character keeps the relationship mobile and adds value to any relationship. Character grows how it is fed and cannot be fabricated. For this same reason, it is that much more difficult to bend character after a certain age, as it is ingrained in how a human develops. However they are fed, they become a product of that fertilizer.

Again, it is that much more difficult to introduce character nurturing after the fact or by introducing something new. Character is also a key determining factor to the depth of a relationship and especially the emotional maturity. You can see why it would be important to have strong positive characters in a relationship to further invest in its longevity. Character is not a latent but an active trait, as it is built on experiences and decisions made by an individual. If you observe less-than-desirable characteristics within yourself or your partner, then I highly recommend you assess the required work to help this person to develop and more so if you can facilitate this growth process. In simplicity, character is what we do when no one is watching.

3. A sense of spiritual well-being, for believers, as a strength, should be nonnegotiable, and, more important, it can be worked on in real time. An adopted definition of spiritual well-being would be a balance between potential and experience where there exists purpose and meaning in life. It is supported by habits of consuming materials of literature and various forms of art and above all believing in a power much greater than any on earth. Believers will share that this experience includes a relationship with God, who is our Creator. Without Him, we would be void, with nothing of substance.

Spiritual well-being includes your mental, emotional, and physical state of being, as all may not be in the same state at the same time.

If you were to evaluate people who identify as being spiritually grounded individuals, you'd admit they express a clear sense of purpose and vision for their lives and are less likely to be dumbfounded by potentially traumatic experiences. There are five main aspects of spiritual and personal wellness: emotional, social, physical, intellectual, and spiritual.

Spiritual wellness also considers the social aspect of a human's existence, which accounts for a large portion of human existence. Some quickly grasp each experience while others need a little time to adjust and capitalize on that experience. Whether your partner is an introvert or extrovert, how would you go about assigning said trait or personality as a strength or weakness? Based on that determination, how would you, as individuals and as a unit, go about catering to your well-being?

Emotional wellness has to do with relaxation, stress reduction, and the development of inner strength. If you are attentive to both the positive and negative feelings, you will be better able to know how to understand and manage these emotions. Emotional wellness also inspires self-care.

Social wellness involves building relationships as well as fostering a genuine connection around you. Social wellness has to do with the relationships we have and how we interact with others, especially in our inner circles. Unless you are an extrovert, social wellness can be very difficult to embrace, because it has to do with interacting with people.

In addition, some of the other requirements to achieve social wellness are nurturing and supporting vulnerable relationships. To maintain social wellness, you would have to maintain a healthy lifestyle.

Social wellness is important because healthy relationships are a vital part of health. A sustainable network will attract people who are sociable and entertaining. Healthier social networks spark life in the immune system so it has the ability to fight off infectious diseases. Also, because of the day-to-day stresses, social wellness must be a part of your schedule. It would be advantageous for both partners to get involved in some form of social wellness practice.

Physical wellness is also never overstated because it maintains your body. This analysis can help you to identify and appreciate the correlations between the mind and the body and how both need to be equally healthy for you to be at your best or trying to improve your best. Your physical health improves as it works as it should and has endless benefits for you. Here are some perfect examples of the link between the mind and the body: smoking and your mood, stress and your ability to manage conflict. And that is just to name two. These are among the most common based on my observations.

Intellectual wellness speaks to the constant stimulation of your brain by introducing new thoughts and new information and forming new habits because of this information. Intellect requires flexibility to remain healthy, and a healthy mind builds a healthier self. That would be the self you present in your relationship. This wellness also helps to develop society.

Spiritual wellness encompasses all of the above and quoting from Proverbs 3:7–8 (NKJV): "Do not be wise in your eyes, Fear the Lord and depart from evil." I must hasten to say that spiritual health and wellness is a journey and not a destination that remains stagnant. In other words, you must continuously work on yourself. A state of spiritual well-being helps you be a better human, which is reflected through compassion, humility, and the lack of fear—or less fear the more your work on your wellness. It is through the manifestation of this journey to wellness that one's temperament changes over time.

Embarking on this journey also is truly one of the healthier ways to transform one's character and reaps the more fulfilling rewards. The Bible teaches that the benefits of spirituality are compassion, love, forgiveness, joy, and fulfillment.

The question you may be asking is how much emphasis you should place on spiritual wellness, considering its strength when applied to the relationship you look forward to having.

4. Appreciation and affection are a demonstration of one's acceptance and appreciation of another and take many forms. I would expand this to say not only is this paying attention to your spouse but also to details on matters important to you and your spouse. Depending on your partner, the emphasis may

not be on displaying this affection publicly, but it never hurts, and once you're into it, it would come naturally regardless of where you may be. Affection and attention should be considered and weighed as such, as the lack of the same is what I would define as weaknesses existing within a relationship. Encourage appreciation and attention at all costs.

WEAKNESSES

Here are just a few hallmark traits that should raise red flags. You should work on them as soon as possible. I would hasten the same concepts used to assess strengths should conversely be used for assessing weaknesses. As a rule, I caution you not to use the physical appearance or personality of your spouse to judge him or her, especially as a weakness. It can be a plus but cannot be based solely on these factors. Identifying your spouse's weaknesses also requires a cross-examination. Whether you can compromise or work with your partner on these weaknesses and try converting them to strengths, the decision is yours:

1. Oversharing too soon—I mean during dating or courtship—is a weakness. I think the pertinent information should not be given out too soon, regardless. Pertinent information should be guarded and not flippantly handed out to all and sundry, especially when dating multiple partners. I am referring to information such as date of birth, address, or ID that may make you vulnerable if used with ill intent by the person you may be dating or someone else he or she may have shared that information with. Not to worry, this can be worked on. I caution, however, that once you share the information, you cannot unshare it. That's it.

Too many women express their weakness at the very onset of their relationship, because they are afraid of losing their partner's interest. Both partners need to exercise discernment, and in case you doubt that you can trust him or her, follow your gut instinct, that first inclination you may have when you hear, see, or think about something or someone. Your instinct has been around forever; you can trust it.

2. Low self-esteem is also a weakness. How an individual values him- or herself is usually apparent, unless the person is putting on an elaborate show of faux low self-esteem, which is its own drama. But I digress. Classic manifestations of low self-esteem include a constant need for reassurance for everything, wanting to know if everything he or she does and says is "correct" or "acceptable." If left unchecked, can unravel any progress you may be trying to work on in your relationship. I use this opportunity to reemphasize that working on each other only helps the relationship, and there is no way to work on the relationship without working on yourself.

3. Substance abuse is when someone overindulges in an addictive substance, especially alcohol or drugs. It is no longer recreational and occasional. Statistically, people with substance addiction would have developed said habit in their teens. You would have to consider how you would thrive with a substance-addicted spouse.

Also be cautious if your "recreational user" of a spouse habitually seeks the high from alcohol or drugs, especially when stressed. That also is a habit in the making, and soon enough, at the slightest hint of strain, the brain, just doing what it has always done, craves this high that it was always fed in the past. This habit has biological, emotional, and mental implications for the body. Substance abuse brings damage to relationships and families. Use of narcotics, such as codeine and hydrocodone, is on the rise. Anyone who is preparing him- or herself for a long-term relationship should reconsider if there is evidence of substance abuse.

In many instances, people have used substance abuse as a substitute to bring calm to themselves and their relationships. In other news, people consumed substances to deflate or escape their problems. Regrettably, prolonged substance abuse translates to diseases like cancer, cardiac problems, respiratory problems, and liver damage, just to name a few. Understandably, in some cases, substance abuse is hereditary, and despite the person's circumstances, he, or she must be treated with care.

4. People should be able to apologize. Again, there are some habits or actions that are best addressed as soon as they arise instead of waiting on more occasions, which again is just habit formation for the brain.

Apologizing should not be required on the premise of condemnation for a wrong that was done but more in acknowledging an error and taking the necessary steps to curtail a repeat in the future. Apologizing to your partner is one of the greatest assets in your relationship. Because the best of us will make mistakes from time to time, I always share with my congregants, young and old alike, that an apology is never complete with just words but must be accompanied consistently by rehabilitative actions, making amends with your partner.

Never think that apologizing is a form of debasement, shame, or degradation, but see it as a form of restoration. The opposite would be to be smug and refuse to apologize, which instead serves an injustice to the relationship. Apologies should never be a form of manipulation but should be genuine when expressed.

You must decide how mistakes will be treated, as strikes against each other or opportunities to learn from. First and foremost, you must decide this before you can decide how to treat them. However, that only addresses how one partner reacts when the other makes a misstep/mistake. The flip side to that coin is the partner who made said misstep or mistake and his or her compulsion to either acknowledge the error and his or her regret to his or her spouse, simply ignore it, or, worse, refuse to acknowledge the pain or discomfort it may have caused his or her partner. Therein lies the crux of a bigger problem. I would say, in the first instance, try to ascertain with said spouse what he or she believes an apology looks like and clear up any misconceptions or unclear expectations. If it continues after that, then it is a clear strike against the relationship.

Let me reemphasize that apologies don't always include the actual scripted words "I am sorry." Your spouse may not say the actual words but may take action to communicate his or her regret and try to ease your pain and discomfort subsequently. It would be a good start to develop your language, including apologizing.

> 5. Another red flag is disliking a spouse's family—*without provocation*, simply meaning if your spouse's family members express their disapproval of any manifested decisions you may make in your relationship, then nothing is wrong with healthy and firm boundaries. Otherwise, if there was no provocation, then being cordial enough should not be so hard. You are important to your spouse, but especially if your spouse is family-oriented, so is his or her family. Being selfish will not add any value to you since everyone is always looking for affirmation. It would be unfair to force your spouse to choose without reasonable grounds. This will require a healthy dose of compromise, depending on the situation.

In essence, without provocation, there should be no reason not to be amiable with your in-laws. It may just be that they will need your help but hesitate to request the same and vice versa. As the Bible encourages, if possible, be at peace with all people, and that includes your soon to-be extended family. Remember, what goes around comes around.

> 6. An untamed tongue is a weakness. The tongue, though just a small muscle, can inflict deep wounds, so you would understand why an untamed, uncontrolled tongue would be classified as a weakness. Like all weaknesses, there are always opportunities to curtail the same and even turn it into a strength. James 3:6 (NKJV) says, "The tongue is a fire, a world of iniquity. The tongue is so set among our members that it defiles the whole body and sets on fire, the course of nature, and it is set on fire by

hell." Simply, the untamed tongue can set a course of irreversible and untold grief for those it is laid against. So, we see that with an untamed tongue, relationships can be destroyed, and either party becomes vulnerable.

Verse 8 goes on to say, "That no man can tame the tongue. It is an unruly evil, full of deadly poison." Again, life and death lie in the power of the tongue, so be guided. Taming the tongue entails restraint and control, and those are essential traits for a long-term commitment.

In essence, admit weaknesses up front and see them as opportunities for growth.

OPPORTUNITIES

Getting right into it, the following are opportunities for a partner or spouse:

1. Be sociable. *Sociable* means having social intelligence, which translates to being able to adapt to different social environments without causing much friction. Being sociable is not the same as being extroverted, but simply means being hospitable or appreciating extended hospitality. Being sociable is all about adjusting your attitude based on the altitude of the situation.

No one wants to date someone acts inhumanely or selfishly. Everyone is looking for someone who is amicable or has a cordial attitude. In this case, attitude determines altitude. It is through being sociable that your attitude will most be on display, and this can have implications for your relationship.

2. Compatibility is such an underutilized screener. It calls for an old saying: "A square peg cannot fit in a round hole." Compatibility is just that. If a relationship feels like there is no common ground or fit, then you may just not be compatible, and compatibility is a staple of a successful long-term relationship. If

both partners are essentially different, then without any form of compromise in any way, minimizing discomfort to either partner, then it is an exercise in futility.

Conversely, if you find someone with whom there is less friction, then it does do something good for the relationship. This brings peace, joy, and fulfilment. Be patient with yourself. Remember, a relationship is not to be rushed.

3. Magic words still work! Yes, you read that right. Simple yet grossly underrated are *please* and *thank you*. You may think it is basic manners, but newsflash, manners also apply to your relationship. You being intimate with the person does not disqualify him or her from common courtesy and manners, and they are usually well received. It communicates respect, appreciation, and gratitude, all of which are important in your relationship every day. Remember, words can make or break relationships.

Another example of magic words is *I am sorry I hurt you*. It is especially phrased to focus on the action and not condemning the person who made such an action. It is fashioned to defuse a situation, heated argument, disagreement, and so on. One point to note with magic words is they must be articulated as sincerity verbalized. This means your partner should feel your appreciation or regret, and that is the power of words. Don't worry; opportunities abound for using magic words, and they cannot be overused. The magic word has the potential to cancel, hurt, or even change the landscape in a relationship. Every opportunity should be considered to use magic words. There is an old song written by Paul Anka, "Don't Gamble With Love" with a portion of the following lyrics, "Don't gamble with love, it's only for fools so play by the rules don't gamble with love"

4. Be an educated lover. There is always room for learning, and even your relationship is a learning journey you take with the partner you choose for however long you choose. It cannot be overstated how important constant edification of the self is in a relationship. It makes all the difference. Many people look for love in diverse places, such as the park, clubs, baseball games, or even church without being educated in the subject matter. Thus they make frequent mistakes. Prior to dating, it is advisable that a good source of education and edification is paramount, preferably through a Christian counselor, trained both in psychology and the word of God. If you are reluctant to do self-education, chances are your relationship will meet its demise quickly.

THREATS

In essence, a threat is anything in any form that is intended to inflict pain, injury, damage, or any other form of hostility to someone. This can either be done without provocation or in retaliation. Threats take many forms and are not always initially physical. They just manifest physically, and sometimes that is the only way the threat is realized. Intimidation is also another form of threat, and I am going to list a few basic threats to any well-meaning and well-intended relationship.

1. Previous relationships' interference—exes are always a sore topic in relationships and obviously pose a direct threat if left unattended. There is no hard rule, but some guidelines include setting your boundaries pertaining to exes, honoring the boundaries you set, and always paying attention to your partner's actions. Guard your partner from outside influence by paying close attention to sudden changes, such as attitudes, mood, and personality, while giving your partner the benefit of the doubt in the first instance and having a frank, though possibly uncomfortable conversation about his or her exes.

This is even more of an important conversation when the lives of innocent children are involved, whether both parents have joint custody, there is a custody battle, or one partner has given up his or her parental rights. Your role is in supporting your partner. Road maps are established to navigate one's direction to the intended destiny. Partners would need to redirect their exes map so as not to end up in the same destination to bring pitfalls to either relationship.

Be wary of how you are introduced to your partner's ex and vice versa. It sounds uncomfortable, but I recommend having the exes conversation as soon as possible to get a feel for the relationship with the exes. Sparks in some of the relationships between exes are synonymous to the restoration of past relationships. Sparks should not be left unnoticed at any cost. Every action creates a reaction; hence transparency needs to be the highest priority. Silence gives either partner the power to do whatever pleases him or her and creates doubt and suspicion in the other person.

2. Lack of trust—I repeat, do not proceed unless you have addressed the matter and have a clear path on how to start building that trust and a way to measure that trust is being built. There is no meaningful relationship without each partner being able to rely on the virtue, character, and word of his or her partner to act within the best interests of the relationship. If trust needs to be repaired in a relationship, that for all intents and purposes was on a good path before the misstep, if it was not on purpose, then one can care for the rebuilding of that trust as one cares for and nurtures a newborn.

Both partners would need to be cognizant that the healing process comes with some flashbacks, triggered by certain actions and words, which transport his or her partner back in time, back to that traumatic moment, for him or her too, when he or she realized the trust was waning, especially when it was unexpected.

I recommend keeping it simple and straightforward on such a fickle matter as trust. It is hard to build and so easy to lose. Be so straightforward that it is almost second nature to

- speak the truth and fast, even when confronted
- do not take each other for granted and strive to be fair considering the circumstances
- forgive actively, once you decide to move past it

See a marriage counselor. It is healthy to do so throughout the course of the relationship, where applicable. Counselors are not only for when you have decided that you have given up and you basically want a third party to help you to change your mind.

Today, with technology, where transparency is concerned, cell phone use has been a sore topic, even in some seemingly stable relationships. Have an open policy about cell phone use and what the boundaries will be.

All round, abide by the rule of thumb: prevention is better than cure.

If we are human, we can benefit from the SWOT analysis. I reemphasize that all I have listed you and your partner should explore, even if the information may not suit your relationship and its circumstances currently. The only priority you should have is the shared goals in your relationship, and in order to stay true to them, you must be willing to accept that those priorities from time to time may change. For example, if a billionaire is ill, his primary concern is no longer his wealth and status; instead, if he wants to live, his priority is rerouted to preserving his health in all ways possible. Your relationship is no different.

I close the SWOT analysis chapter because it is time to get to work. Once you embark on this exercise with your partner, I caution that you give equal attention to all four while deliberating. Once you have identified what you need to work on, then you and your partner can decide how to prioritize that list; it is also healthy, if over time, as a couple, your priorities must change. Again, weaknesses and threats can be transformed with the right approach, so tread intelligently and purposefully. The devil is in the details, so pay attention, and once your goal isn't equally fulfilling, then you should welcome the journey.

8. MENTAL READINESS: AM I REALLY MENTALLY READY?

Mental readiness is the crux. It is the ability to remain focused. Mental readiness in the context of a relationship that is intended to be long term is important. Taking the steps to achieve mental readiness includes addressing your fears, and that process is best started as soon as possible. Fear has the potential to destroy your dreams and put your life on hold. If your life is consumed with and ruled by fear, then you should not consider pursuing a relationship just yet. The essence of being in a relationship is the conquering of your fears; it is inevitable.

Depending on who you are dating, the fear is also very present earlier on in the relationship. This emotion can be used constructively if addressed honestly, but otherwise, it can be destructive if left to fester. The fear of making mistakes, for example, is a common fear in relationships, and it requires a sense of presence to address this fear constructively while not neglecting other areas of your life.

Fear or no fear, it is never a good start to cast blame when things go wrong in the relationship. This, in fact, signifies immaturity, which left unchecked, as we explored in the previous chapter, is a weakness and a possible insider threat to the relationship. It is always good to continually assess the relationship and determine what you can work on, but I encourage restraint from doing so by casting or assigning blame to a partner.

Mental readiness should be continuously reviewed, and a simple checklist should form a starting point, a practice for both men and women. A mental checklist can serve as a point of reference but should be adjustable based on reality. For long-term relationships, a few staples are character, morality, and ethics.

Once you have this checklist, you can delve a little further into the following:

1. Am I mature enough for a relationship?
2. Am I ready to stop jumping from relationship to relationship?
3. Does timing really matter to me?
4. Have I learned from my past relationships?
5. Did I envision the right partner for me to purposefully engage with?

1. Being mature enough—an underlying problem in relationships is that mental maturity is lacking, as it was not actively sought by individuals. Pursuing a relationship calls for that mental readiness, and maturity can help the process. It is a sign of immaturity if you or your partner continuously criticizes each other with the intent to erode the other's confidence. It would be pertinent to not only choose your words carefully when offering a critique but also to choose your words carefully in general.

Good intentions start with the words, which means both partners have the responsibility to examine their thoughts before uttering them. It erodes all confidence if you hurt the person you intend to say "I do" to with your words. Always be on your spouse's side in that you are continuously supportive of everything that makes him or her a better person and ultimately a better partner. You should take pride in helping your partner realize his or her greatness. You will need a sense of direction to take you to that place. This brings us to the next point.

It is also a sign of immaturity if you or your partner does not have the capacity for long-term planning, which is also crucial in any relationship or commitment. If you fail to plan, you might as well plan to fail. Planning essentially speaks to how adept you are at planning. James 1:8 (NKJV) states, "He is a double-minded man, unstable in all his ways." He would be nothing less than a ship without a sail, in the middle of a sea that is boisterous. The sailor would have no control over the direction the ship takes. The same can be said of relationships where there is no sense of direction whatsoever.

Mental readiness is also not playing the "blame shame game." This means no constant blaming of each other, based on actions, clear limitations, and so on. It is counterproductive to the relationship. Yes, taking responsibility for missteps must be encouraged; however, there should be no blaming or shaming that partner; efforts should instead be made to move past this event or action and to try to help your partner to move past his or her weakness.

Gossiping, in its purest form and for the sake of gossiping, is also a sign of immaturity, and if left unattended, it can have serious negative implications for your relationship. Fact-checking is always good, but taking pleasure out of discussing the ins and outs of others' lives, as unrelated to you, definitely is a red flag. This is exceptionally so when the details being disclosed, unrelated to anyone else, are private details of the relationship. If left unchecked, especially if your partner has consternations, it may strike marks against your relationship and erode your partner's trust in you in appreciating and honoring the sanctity of the relationship.

A partner who gossips is at risk of betraying the trust of his or her partner. If you observe that your partner is prone to gossiping, then in a way that your partner can appreciate and reinforces values against this practice, you should address the issue.

Allow me to flip the script and paint a picture of what a mature relationship would look like. It is one where both partners speak to each other with kind regard and respect, absent of habitual use of obscene language. It is a relationship where there is verbal and nonverbal admiration between partners. It is one where plans are put in place for the future, and both partners take the necessary steps to fulfill each one of those plans. One who gossips will ultimately destroy a relationship. It is therefore necessary to confront the issue, making sure your partner is aware of your concerns. Mental maturity can easily be identified by several factors in a relationship.

2. Are you ready to stop jumping from one relationship to the next? Dating multiple people is not abnormal, as long as both partners concede that that is what they are doing. Multiple dating is establishing friendship and getting to know each other better. Otherwise, it is reckless and involves implications of not just one or two people but potentially more, depending on how many partners one may be dating.

Personally, I have observed and conceded to myself that the advent of technology and culture have all played major roles in the dramatic shift seen in younger generations as they navigate the dating space and sometimes create their own rules regarding the subject. In this century, it is more about instant gratification. Two centuries ago, lawlessness was at a minimum, and so the human minds were much eviler and more conniving. Proverbs 14:34 (NKJV) declares, "Righteousness exalts a nation, but sin is a reproach to any people." Noted, all nations are included in this context. It's pathetic when we observe the operation of our twenty-first-century so-called lovers.

If I may comment, about twenty years ago, there were more stable and happy relationships. The differences and results are vast when looking at these two separate generations, and so are the lifestyle choices. As for the dietary choices, the nutritionist could not have articulated it better by informing us that proper dieting and exercising are necessary for good health, long life, and everything in between. I look at the mass production of food that the younger generation, millennials, are consuming, which lacks the dietary requirements to nourish both their bodies and minds. Consequently, there will be noticeable differences in their behaviors and thought processes, based on dietary differences that provide little to no nourishment. Poor diet has effects much like substance abuse; they both leave your faculties impaired and cause greater strain when certain performance is required.

There are also more TV, internet, media, and billboard influences now than in the boomer generation, all of which subliminally impress on our younger generations to act differently. As a father of three millennials, I am acutely aware of the minute differences, and it takes some amount of balancing to ensure that all involved remain respectable and have healthy boundaries.

3. Does timing really matter? Time matters if you are on a clock. Time matters, for instance, if you are getting older and are more susceptible to the pressure placed on you by society, which says you must have a family by a certain age. Time may also run out on you if by a certain age, your reproductive system also beckons with the ticking clock, and this applies to both sexes. Unless it is a situation like this, then time should only matter as much as you decide that it does.

Time only matters when you have a clear sense of direction and of what you are looking for. Time, however, I caution again, is fluid. You must be able to strike a balance between your pending anxieties and not acting prematurely, which may have consequences down the line. Time, however, does not matter if you have no concept or appreciation for it. Time doesn't matter if you do not make use of it, no matter how young or old you are. The concept of timing in relationships is also different, based on, of course, who is in the relationship and, in a broader context, the society and culture.

For instance, in some cultures, it is considered the norm for there to be a specific period of dating or looking for a suitable partner, potentially dating after selecting from a pool of potentials, after which it is a series of negotiations with elders on the potential couple's behalf, as is the case in India, where arranged marriages are part of the culture. Potential partners use their older relatives to advertise their profiles through various media, after which, these multiple potential partners are then vetted by the relatives. These relatives go on to set up meetings for both prospective partners. After all the vetting, there is an opportunity for friendship to blossom.

Interestingly, India also has among the lowest rates of divorce, despite most of said marriages having been arranged. There are three factors that drive positive outcomes from arranged marriages in the Indian culture:

1. removing the difficult aspects from the decision-making process;
2. only one pool of suitable candidates to choose from, and
3. the vetting process further refines the searchable pool.

Where there is no interference from families or bonds that were made centuries ago for descendants to adhere to, there is free choice. Free-choice marriage will always be more complicated, demanding more time and energy to locate the right partner. People rely on love and its various forms of expression. This context, however, does not take into consideration the topic of dowries. This, in the most traditional of senses, was intended to serve as a foundation for the new couple. This dowry is then returnable to the bride's family if the marriage ends without producing a son. Again, I am not making any personal recommendations; I'm simply stating what has worked.

4. Did I learn from the previous relationship? Depending on the person, this answer may range from total disregard to the opposite, where there is still too much regard for the relationship that has ended. I have now concluded in the existence of what I term relationship insanity, which is where the same people

make the same decisions about the same matters and yet expect different results. This toxic cycle could be because of low self-esteem and lack of confidence in one's ability to make decisions and be confident in them. This leads to accepting the mediocre as one's high standard. These people fall into the category of succumbing to pressure from different factions, so they would rather convince themselves of being satisfied in a mediocre and unsatisfying relationship than be single. Recognizing your value or worth will help you to maneuver out of toxic cycles.

Philippians 4:13 (NKJV) reminds us "I can do all things through Christ who strengthens me". There are, however, a few ways you can discern and break this toxic cycle of relationship insanity:

1. Deduce if the feeling is based on love or infatuation.
2. Discern the habits that you have formed and those that have been detrimental to your relationship by doing a reality check. This, of course, will break the cycle of denial, thus causing critics to stop their investigation.
3. You instinctively know when something doesn't feel right. Once you admit this, it is important to consider your health and make wise and healthy decisions pertaining to that relationship. Your health should take priority, and it requires maturity to admit when a relationship is not good for you and your health, both physical and mental.

Hitching up with a serial cheater to produce children out of wedlock and to be in denial of a prevailing abuser are nonstarters for anyone with a vision for the future. Every relationship should have a standard of decency and a couple who take pride in their relationship. Otherwise, relationship insanity will kick in.

Every decision needs your consent, and every action needs your input. I reiterate the importance of assessing your own habits and their implications. Are you yielding your required results? Are you shocked by said results? It is almost akin to having unprotected sex with multiple partners and then being surprised at contracting a sexually transmitted infection (STI), just for an example. Lamenting over such an irreversible event is not preventative for the future unless you act.

The choices you make today will affect your tomorrow. The longer you take, for instance, to end a toxic relationship while repeating the same patterns of thought, choices, and behaviors, the more contempt you will have, not just for your partner but also for yourself when you admit this is not the relationship you want. The longer you remain in a toxic relationship, the more you are being exposed to self-inflicted wounds.

5. Did I envision the right partner? If you can envision something, you can have it soon enough. Every potential partner has a right to the specifics of what they are looking for in a relationship and their soon-to-be spouses. But this process requires due diligence and a firm grasp of reality, especially when your vision looking to be materializing. Going on a wild goose chase would put you in a nonproductive position, thus not accomplishing your desired goal. Not envisioning the right person can be a painful exercise since everyone looks for the best of partners. Unless you paint a picture of what you are envisioning, you may never arrive at your destination. Some factors you would need when looking for a partner entirely based on your preferences include his or her personality, height, complexion, ethnicity, social standing, financial stability, family background, religious affiliations, and the like. Again, this depends on what you want out of the relationship.

Many look for partners with some amount of compatibility since the law of attraction states that "like attracts like." This means if you are insecure, your tendency will be becoming attracted to an insecure person and vice versa. Those people who love and value themselves will also attract each other. Christian practice is to be equally yoked together. Second Corinthians 6:14 (NKJV) reminds us to "Do not be unequally yoked together with unbelievers. For what fellowship has righteousness with lawlessness? And what communion light with darkness?" This simply means choosing a partner of the same faith and Christian values.

All this speaks to the mental readiness and mental preparation required when contemplating a relationship. It is up to you to broach this topic with your partner or take a break to work on your mental selves before making a commitment.

9. AM I PHYSICALLY READY FOR A RELATIONSHIP?

A profound question to as oneself is "Am I physically ready?" What constitutes physical readiness? The simple answer is you are responsible for your health, making sure it is unparalleled at all times.

Procrastination, better known as the thief of time, can lead to our demise if we refuse to act accordingly. Often, we ignore abnormal feelings, symptoms that point to a disease or disorder, but I daresay every unusual pain or symptom should be taken seriously.

Physical readiness plays a crucial role in the development of any relationship. It also gives a picture of the five senses and their functionality and of the human body as a whole. If any of these senses are off, the relationship can be jeopardized. Your health should be taken seriously, especially when you are about to take your relationship to the ultimate level.

In 3 John 1:3 (NKJV), the Bible declares, "Beloved, I pray that you may prosper in all things and be in health, just as your soul prospers."

This, among many other scriptures in the Bible, refers specifically to the believer's physical health. It would be an understatement to say that health plays a minor role in a relationship, and this is the onus of both partners, regardless of their sex, to prioritize their health.

Despite all the support systems one may have, one still does not delegate the responsibility for one's health; it is solely his or hers. Annual checkups are usually understated and most definitely overlooked; consequently, if left unchecked for years, one may be in for a health surprise or scare. I have known several individuals who lost their lives because of being neglectful of their health but not their wealth. But make no mistakes, logically speaking, your health is your wealth. It means that relationship or no, you must place emphasis on your physical well-being to plan and act accordingly.

It helps to be conscious of your body and the subtle warning signs it may give you before it becomes too severe. You must be so in tune with your body that any slight changes, whether improvement or lack thereof, you would know.

I would daresay I know a thing or two pertaining to keeping tabs on your health within the context of a relationship and doing so in a way that meaningfully includes your partner. I keep a few devices around just to have an idea before making that trip to the doctor. I call it my health check kit. It includes the following:

1. Sphygmomanometer to check my blood pressure
2. Stethoscope to routinely monitor my heart rate
3. Suction device to get rid of excess blood or secretions.
4. Thermometer (yes, I had mine before COVID prompted a stock up in households that can stock up; I have been routinely checking my temperature)

As you can see, most of the tools in my kit are to check on what is happening inside the body, not just on the outside. Looking healthy on the outside does not mean that one is 100 percent healthy. On that note, exercise alone to tone muscles only works on strength and endurance, and that only accounts for a part of your physical health. I have also noticed that women tend to be more open and attentive to their overall health; men, for some reason, refuse to admit a symptom or even a condition until it poses dire threats to their lives. I denounce this practice and discourage it on so many levels, not simply because you hurt in silence when the matter could have been addressed but because it is unfair to put your spouse through a scare that you knew was coming, especially if said spouse has been encouraging you to take your health seriously. Think about it. But ironically, don't just think about yourself but also those who care about you.

Dieting, which to an extent is based on the needs of the body, should be a way of life. You should not simply be consuming food that smells great—hence the term *balanced diet*. This simply means you try to cover as much as possible and monitor your portions. A healthy diet is good for your mental and physical health; it can reduce the risk of obesity, heart disease, diabetes, hypertension, depression, and cancer. You should eat to gain energy through proper nutrients. Each excess portion has its own risks.

Any dietician will recommend that one's balanced diet have healthy doses of carbohydrates, proteins, fat, fiber, vitamins, minerals, and water. Most of our diet is unbalanced with too many carbs or too much protein. The trick in balancing your diet is watching the ratio of your portions. For instance, traditionally, some dishes have pasta, rice, chicken, and potatoes (carb heavy) as opposed to chicken, pasta or rice, and vegetables (which eliminates one of the carbohydrates).

A balanced diet looks a little something like the following:

1. Carbohydrates accounting for 45 to 55 percent of one's daily calorie intake and coming through grains, wheat, oats, rice, flour, pasta, noodles, potatoes, yam, fruits, and sugar. Carbohydrates are the main ingredient to give you energy.

2. Protein accounting for 10 to 35 percent of one's daily calorie intake, which consisting of meat, fish, eggs, nuts, soybeans, and pulses. Proteins have many benefits, one of which is used to build tissue growth and maintenance thus increasing your body's needs.

3. Fats accounting for 20 to 35 percent, consists of nuts, seeds, plants, oils, and dairy products. Fats are essential for energy storage and hormone production.

Other dietary essentials include the following:

1. Fiber, had through beans, vegetables, fruits, oats, whole grains, brown rice, nuts, and seeds. Fiber helps to regulate blood sugar and gut health.

2. Vitamins and minerals from specific vegetables, meats, nuts, and seeds. They are vital for metabolism regulation, cell growth, and other biochemical functions.

3. Water to ensure the body is constantly hydrated. Though the best way to consume it is by drinking solely water, other beverages can play a role in hydration.

All the above play a role in providing a recommended daily calorie intake. If you go by the broadly recommended 2,500 calories for men and 2,000 calories for women, these should give you a clear idea of what the requirements would be for each essential and, of course, how much would be classified as too much. Please bear in mind a few factors affect this formula, such as, age, sex, job description, growth, any underlying health issues, and so on.

Now remember when I stated that exercise alone cannot guarantee health? That is the truth. But if balanced with dieting and adequate rest, among other practices, exercising will do what it was meant to: revitalize and rejuvenate the body. Exercising is a staple in the battle against heart disease and depression. Not to mention studies show evidence of lower risks of such complications in people who lead active lifestyles.

Because it has been proven that physical inactivity, smoking, and obesity are modifiable risk factors for death, it is important to practice frequent exercise. Physical exercise produces a relaxed mood and keeps depression at bay. God wants us to live stress-free lives. It is clear that those who exercise and are actively engaged on a regular basis are much more productive. It is also stated that serotonin and energy levels in the brain increase mental clarity. Those who are inactive will have the tendency of staggering cognition.

I daresay it is recommended that health be prioritized in a relationship and actively pursued, not just talked about. Yes, I cannot tell you what to do; I can only encourage you to do what would be beneficial to you and your spouse. Learn to be spontaneous and creative on the health journey with your spouse. An annual checkup could be treated like a date. More couples would do it, and each partner could decide how involved in the process he or she would like his or her partner to be.

All of the above are preferred actions you should take before entering a relationship, but it is never too late to start. Consider your health an investment and be realistic. Would you want to invest in a bad deal? Understandably as well, some jobs rely on good physical strength.

All this is in response to your self-assessment of your physical well-being when prospecting for a relationship. By the same measure you would assess your potential partner, expect no less of yourself. You also must ensure that you are considering your relationship for the right reasons.

Another factor to consider is the male partner needs to consider his future responsibility because of the mandate demanding his ability to work. No potential lover or wife wants to date a man who is unemployed. Too many women allow a nonworking man to invade their lives with promises of getting a job, which never happens. Ladies should evaluate themselves and see their potential going beyond their imagination. Ladies should see themselves as overcomers and not failures. God's word states in Philippians 4:13 (NKJV), "I can do all things through Christ who strengthens me." Ladies, look in a mirror and tell yourself you are valuable and priceless. Hold your head high like the queen you are and wait until God finds the king for you. Men need to have a vision before initiating a relationship. Having a vision would allow them to make decisions that could effectuate change in many areas. Young men should be versatile, not only to have a degree, but in addition learning a skill, such as carpentry, masonry, plumbing, electrical and so on. Having multiple skills plus a degree would be of advantage, especially if you are pursuing marriage. This strategy will mitigate financial burden at some point in the relationship.

Another aspect of assessing physical readiness is how you handle stress, especially when you are under pressure, as that dictates how your body responds to the stress. Stress can be inevitable and can be brought on by many different factors, like jobs, inadequate rest, and lack of support on your part. Granted, preparing to say "I do" has its own stress and understandably so. You may feel a different type of nervousness, being tense or scared, and the list goes on, but that is normal. In this case, instead of panicking, plan with a strategy, get proper sleep, find time for relaxation, and indulge in physical exercise. If all else fails, speak to a stress therapist. Investing in your physical health goes a long way in preserving the sanctity of your relationship, especially if you plan to say, "I do."

Your physical health also has implications for your ability to romance and sexually please your spouse. Instances of physical limitations include erectile dysfunction, which occurs when a man is unable to get an erection. This condition is sometimes treatable; however, it depends on the root cause. This can then lead to strains in the relationship, eroding self-confidence and stress on both partners. There are a range of home remedies and medications that can address or alleviate erectile dysfunction. They include the following: maca, tongkat ali, L-arginine, *Tribulus terrestris*, ginseng, and horny goat weed, with popular brands such as Ergot, Ageless Male, or 3x Calibers. Some even go to the lengths of shock wave therapy.

As a practicing counselor for years and a husband, it is alarmingly unsurprising that a large percentage of men across the States have various degrees of erectile dysfunction and are also at significantly increased risk as they age. It is especially more prevalent between the ages thirty-six years and forty-five years. The sexual response cycle has four phrases: excitement, plateau, orgasm, and resolution. Based on the reported percentage of both males and females who encounter this problem, it would be accurate to say that some are still embarrassed about approaching the subject.

Imagine having had numerous conversations with your spouse, leading up to marriage, about sex, and yet on your honeymoon, you are surprised to realize that your husband has an erectile problem, one that could have been treated before, except your spouse was not forthcoming with the situation so that you could arrive at a solution faster. Then you are let down at the last minute.

Again, I encourage men, make it a norm to talk about your physical health, the basic things; once you have a healthy concept of sharing, then it becomes easier to share the more intimate details, even the embarrassment you can get past once you have the will to fight for your relationship and your spouse.

Conversely, women who are impacted by lack of sexual stimulation have this symptom because of consequences of diabetes, heart disease, hormonal imbalances, neurological diseases, menopause, chronic illnesses, or side effects of contraceptives, hormonal medication, or antidepressants.

Physical health issues manifest in many ways, and the sooner the conversation starts, the easier it is to manage any challenges that may arise later in the relationship. Everything I mentioned is part of a conversation you would need to have with your spouse, but before you can have that conversation with someone else, you must be willing to admit this to yourself and be open to the possibility of having this confrontation someday, no matter how uncomfortable the topic may seem.

Footnote: your physical health has many and sometimes even grave implications, so it is essential to start, even with the smallest, first step. Be sure to remember you are responsible for your health.

10. AM I FINANCIALLY READY FOR A RELATIONSHIP?

Marriage is a big decision, and since it is usually a monumental stop on a long-term journey, it is important to have the "F" talk, especially when there are times that despite the intense feelings, there is a stall in taking the final step in saying "I do." Finances should not be the only topic, but they should be included in the conversation. Again, it is all about balance. Gone are the days when family members would support the union on this special occasion, especially financially. Cards must be laid on the table from as early as possible if I may.

The wedding scene has also transformed to accommodate the changing ways marriage and wedding planning have been presented. Currently, almost everything can be rented for a ceremony, as opposed to the traditional way of marking the occasions and following certain traditions like storing wedding attire and even trying it on later in the marriage. On the subject of traditions' perseveration, my wife and I both still have our wedding attire, which we occasionally take out and try on, for laughs of course.

Talking about finances is not just for the big day, but the relationship itself, ultimately leading up to the wedding, the wedding itself, and the journey that begins after marriage. You and your spouse must agree on what constitutes financial readiness and what that looks like at different stages and steps within the relationship.

I hope we can all agree that financial stability should include long-term financial planning and, ideally, multiple streams of income that adequately support one's lifestyle and one's to-be spouse's. Financial stability too is achieved from a place of prudence, the ability to act as carefully with your money as possible.

Here are a few ways that one can assess or ascertain financial readiness.

The first step is to admit your financial position, because money is hard to accumulate but easy to use. If you assess your financial standing and see gaps that need to be filled, then find the desire to fill those gaps; this is called budgeting, and your financial self will thank you for it. Again, your financial position may not solely be represented by liquid assets, meaning money, but it is a good start. Once you have an idea of what you have and, more important, what you will need, if it applies to you, you can now pursue higher levels of education or certification, which may be in the form of a skill, to increase your earning potential.

Do not be discouraged by entry-level positions, such as that of a cashier, waitress, and so on, as there is dignity in honest work. I implore you, however, to dictate your own financial path and work toward it. If nothing else, this pandemic has shown that the most overlooked and discarded have now been revealed as essential, as they are essential to all. Also do not be adamant by working and trying to further your education. Have a clear goal and be willing to endure the time spend to realize that goal.

I am a prime example of this endurance, there are friends and associates of mine, currently in long-term relationships with children and some measure of financial stability. I migrated to the United States more than thirty years ago and had my first job as a messenger in the heart of the city, with my new wife in a rental apartment in Brooklyn. If you can dream it, there is a possibility I have done the job; when I wasn't hopping subways to deliver mail, I was the office custodian, tasked with ensuring the office and the bathroom was clean. Mark you, I already had more than fifteen years of experience in my field of construction, and yet I humbled myself through this job for several years.

Finally, I was able to gain employment in my field of construction, and I was again a custodian. Admittedly, it was a bitter pill to swallow, yet again, even with humility, I did it, in addition to relationship sacrifices like being out early and coming home late at night, during which time my wife would become pregnant and still decide to support me by picking me up from the subway whenever she could. I did not give up. I steadily worked on the goal I had, the goal that my wife and I promised each other, and soon enough, I was attending New York University to satisfy the US's matriculation requirements and to be promoted. In time, I was able to land another job in construction, with more pay, until that company relocated, at which point my then soon-to-be ex-boss gave me all his office furniture, which I stored in our tiny apartment and continued to work for myself. Soon enough, I was able to hire several positions, from office managers to subcontractors, and we had owned our own construction equipment. My goal had to expand after a while to include more space for my work and emancipate it from our family's living room.

My ambitions didn't stop there, as I also had my ambitions in having my own ministry, which I did after eight years of Bible school and earning my degrees all the way to my doctorate in theology. My wife and I can say the time was well spent, and every sacrifice has been rewarded. This is not to say it was without opposition, as I was unwelcomed by my local church and ultimately ordained by another pastor.

One of my favorite topics in the seminary was counseling. My dissertation was on relationships and marriage, which prompted me at the time to write my first book *Twelve Essentials for a Successful Marriage*. Suffice all this to say that regardless of where life may find you right now, you can move ahead. I am a prime example. It is up to you to make each step count on your journey. Both sexes, however, need to have a degree of belief and conviction in themselves and their potential before entering a relationship.

The bottom line is a plan, and, yes, your spouse will not always meet you at your final destination, but it takes you believing in yourself and your ability to achieve your goals before convincing someone to take that journey with you, and even if you find someone who believes in you without much convincing, then still count yourself blessed and favored and continue to work on yourself.

Once you and your spouse agree that financial stability is a shared goal, then you both agree to focus on the goal and endure the distractions and obstacles. Financial goals work best when they are shared as opposed to being used as a dividing wedge between partners. You must embrace that predominantly you will be required to make choices that feel like sacrifices at the time, and it will take the form of recreational activities and some people in your life.

You will find that financial stability is inevitable when you invest your resources and time according to your plans and when you and your partner decide to dedicate yourselves to the relationship and are willing to do whatever it takes to make the relationship work. Sometimes this sacrifice looks like giving up things and people, but more so, it is about adjusting how you use your time and resources. Take me, for instance, and the examples I gave earlier about how I had to work and how long I had to work. There were times when I had to make financial sacrifices and sacrifice my sleep and family time to achieve my goals.

If there is no wedge between you and your partner because of your financial goals, then you will have a better chance at averting financial instability. This instability takes many forms but most definitely includes lack of commitment by one spouse or both spouses, lack of support by either or both spouses when some sacrifices are required, and, most important, complacency.

Another great beginner on the path to financial stability is saving. On this note, you can invest, especially in the age of technology, in inexpensive education that helps you better understand and manage your finances. There are many helpful tools on the market that can help beginners to manage their finances, such as Level Money, Digit Advertising, Bill Guard, Acorns, Good Budget, and more. They will teach you about budgeting, from which you can garner your savings.

If you have poor money management traits or are just bad with spending money, then habitual budgeting can actually help to curb some of these habits and, more so, help you understand the cost of said habits. Here are a few staples in any structured budget that can be adapted by both partners:

- tithes and offering: 10–14%
- mortgage or rent: 20–28%
- groceries: 9–12%
- insurance: 7–11%
- utilities: 4–5%
- child education costs: 2–3%
- investments: 3–4%
- savings: 9–12%
- medical costs and medical emergencies: 3–4%
- clothing: 3–6%
- vacation: 2–3%
- debts: 1–2%
- social activities: 1–2%

- other children's expenses: 1–3%
- miscellaneous expenses: 5–6%

All these expenses should be reflected through receipts, check stubs, pay stubs, and so on to help you keep track of spending and continually assess your budget as a couple, and this should be balanced against all accounts, expenses, and savings alike.

MANAGING YOUR FINANCES

When it comes to managing the finances in a union, one partner can be elected to handle the bills, preferably the spouse who is evidently stronger at money management skills. For me and mine, that partner is my wife. She ensures that we maximize every dollar spent. Both parties would be responsible for their individual spending.

The partner assigned as the stronger money manager should not dictate from this position but should be one who seeks to arrive at a mutually beneficial agreement that oversees the couple's financial bottom line, expenditures, and assessing steps made toward financial goals. Again, prudence is required in this situation, because even though one person is elected to manage the money, the next partner's action can support or hinder the work of the one managing the money.

USE OF FINANCIAL SOFTWARE

Organizing and tracking finances, for beginners, can be done through Excel or QuickBooks. Managing finances can become consuming, understandably with more activity within a couple's budget as well as the many commitments each spouse may have to balance, especially the one keeping track of the finances. Using software helps if the information is accurate.

FINANCIAL GOALS

I have mentioned these goals before, though these take on the specific needs of the individuals in the relationship. Discussing said goals should be at a mutually beneficial time, preferably when the attention of said partner is available. Such a monumental discussion is not ideal for church, on the road, driving, on the phone and so on, where not only can no solution be achieved but your partner's attention may be focused elsewhere. Because it will take some planning, it is best that both parties are relaxed and prepared for the discussion. Have a financial meeting with your spouse today.

DEALING WITH BANK ACCOUNTS

Some couples prefer separate accounts or one partner being the account holder—yes, it occasionally happens. I encourage you from the get-go to separate personal accounts from business accounts, as this safeguard them against any liability on the business front. For instance, I recall years ago, when I fell short of honoring my full business obligations to the IRS, there was no time wasted in them trying to recover the same from my other accounts, until the matter was soon rectified.

A joint account further cements the couple's commitment to take this journey together. Each partner can always have his or her separate account, but the main account, as has worked for me for thirty-plus years, is the joint account, through which most transactions are funneled.

FINANCIAL TRANSPARENCY

Transparency in general is a staple but even more so in financial matters, especially for a couple who are growing and having bolder financial plans and ambitions. Regardless of whether you are going on a financial journey alone, I recommend you be transparent about it, its purpose, if possible. Granted, it could be a secret pool (Susu) for a surprise birthday gift or party for your spouse, but that is short term. You can say something like, "You will see what it is for soon enough." Say something that validates your spouse's concerns.

Each spouse can have his or her personal money, as a gift from his or her spouse or from the family budget, and of course each spouse is free to spend that as he or she wishes. In fact, it is a healthy practice. It applies equally to both parties. Taking it back to the beginning though, back to the time before you both said "I do" and before you opened joint accounts, transparency should be practiced from the beginning. It would be fair to both your relationship and your partner to disclose any debts that you may be entering the relationship with and what plans you have to eliminate those debts, as well as to value your partner's feedback, which leads me to the next point.

One of the greatest enemies to a marriage is credit card debt, especially when undisclosed from the inception of the relationship. Poor handling of credit and credit cards is a natural hindrance to the potential that any relationship may have to thriving. Clearing these debts should be handled strategically, and there must be commitment on both sides. Please refrain from taking your marriage vows of "for better or for worse" out of context.

GETTING OUT OF FINANCIAL DEBT

Money can be a great and healthy motivator; however, if left unchecked, the love of money and being constantly tempted can be unhealthy and become unsustainable sooner or later, regardless of what you are willing to do for that money. Nothing is wrong with wanting more money, but the Bible warns us that the love of money is the root of all evil.

Regardless of this fantasy of money, many are so far on the other end of the spectrum where they are stuck in financial debt. Some reasons for this include poor money management, unemployment, excessive spending, credit debts, and, for believers, lack of tithing; all are seeds from which bad debt can spring. Money should be valued; otherwise, you don't respect something you work so hard to obtain. These habits swiftly can develop into an addiction to spending money in some illogical ways. It is also a culprit of many divorces, as some marriages are not able to recover. Insufficient finance in a relation is one of the key causes of divorce.

The habit of using credit cards is prevalent in the teenage culture. Statistics share with us that more than 60 percent of teenagers have fallen to credit card debt. This subtle and craving habit was initiated by junk mail, where requests are made of you to provide certain information wherein you can in turn get credit in the thousands of dollars, which is appealing to many.

Getting out of financial debt is not easy and, ironically, requires discipline in more ways than acquiring the money in the first place. Honestly, if one was disciplined in the first instance, unless it was an untimely emergency, such debt would not befall that person. I recommend addressing and servicing any financial debt before family planning, simply because once children are in the picture, there can be unprecedented expenses. For believers, we serve a God of order and balance. Financial debts and all the chaos that come with them are the opposite of that.

Here are just a few tips that can help to curtail financial debt:

1. You can never go wrong with cash, as it limits your spending at any given moment and you can monitor how much cash you keep on your person.
2. Minimize the number of credit cards you have. Try to have only one and use it solely for emergencies.
3. Constantly evaluate your spending habits and see where your money is going.
4. Do not be reckless with your money; treat it with respect.
5. Separate your wants from your needs, and evaluate your spending accordingly, preferably before you spend, especially if it wasn't in your budget.

PERSONAL TESTIMONY

My children can attest to me having frank conversations with them about spending and managing credit card spending as early as they were able to understand.

I have gone through six credit cards, leading to near financial ruin. The trick is that more people need to realize that it takes seconds to get into debt, and it may take you years to recover from said possibly impulsive spending. I am of the firm belief that habits are imprinted based on frequency of exposure. I implore not just relationship-hopefuls but also parents to encourage spending habits that won't lead to financial ruin.

For those planning families, 3 John 2 (NKJV) declares, "Beloved I pray that you may prosper in all things and be in health, just as your soul prospers." The scripture in Proverbs 13:22 (NKJV) also encourages, "A good man shall leave an inheritance for his children's children."

Because money is so important, in relationships and out, it is the leading cause in relationship rifts and sometimes leads to divorce. Do not sleep on your financial goals as a couple. Decide on how to treat the subject of money in a relationship and try to honor it; only change it for the better. Trust, again, is hard to earn and easy to destroy. This is even more so in the financial context. People are attached to their money because of the hard work they must do to earn it, and based on said satisfaction and amount, they may not be able to afford mistakes or missteps in poor spending. Please respect your partner's relationship with money.

Trust and transparency should be invested in, in as many areas as possible in your life. This safeguards against financial infidelity, which can quickly erode your relationship when your partner has the misfortune to find out you have been dishonest, deceptive, or abusive about the finances in the relationship or that you are being selfish with your own financial resources.

Financial infidelity should be avoided at the very beginning of the relationship. Whatever financial machines you employ—insurance, investing, and so on—should be entered with mutual agreement between partners as to how they will be handled. For instance, both partners should have a healthy appreciation of not wanting to grow older and find themselves broke; once this agreement is cemented, both partners can work constantly toward this goal. Working as you get older should be a choice, especially if you have a love for what you do and not necessarily a need to sustain yourself.

Especially in the context of finances, four topics must be broached before making that final transition to marriage: handling money, children, religion, and your in-laws on both sides. Once you have agreed on a commitment to each other not to go around discussing your finances with anyone, you can be honest about your current financial position, assets, and debts, both formal and informal, as well as your personal financial goals. I reiterate, I encourage you to not delay this conversation until after marriage, especially if a blended or extended family would be in the works.

Do not commit without all the facts. If you have as many facts as possible and decide to or not to, at least you would have calculated the risks, for instance, accepting knowledge of your spouse having a $20,000 debt. The decision is ultimately yours, all I humbly ask is that you consider the details and seek to know as much as possible before committing to marriage.

Raising a family obviously would impact a couple's finances, and a frank conversation is required as soon as possible. If children are already involved, then a plan to make both relationships work without compromising either would be required. If both partners have no children, then here family planning can take on another meaning. How many children do you want? How will they be raised and educated? Where will they live and so on? It is never too early to have this conversation and of course imagine the clear impact the answers may have on your finances.

Financial readiness will also be impacted by you and your spouse's religious affiliations. I encourage compatibility. This way, both partners are appreciative of the spiritual importance of tithes and offering, for instance, instead of one thinking it is an unnecessary expense. Again, compatibility would be key in being on the same financial page in this scenario.

The last signal of financial readiness is your views on your to-be in-laws and what would be considered healthy financial limits, meaning, after you get engaged or married, does either side of in-laws expect that you would automatically take care of the entire generation? Would you be put out if your spouse constantly lends money to close family and relatives that may not be repaid? All these are real scenarios. Both partners must have a firm grasp of a concept, be willing to share, and agree, granted they may both agree to disagree with my concept, and that is fine—at least they would be one.

The concept is once you get married, your first loyalty is to your spouse; your parents, families, relatives, and so on all come afterward. With this being my concept, I concede that there are fun and healthy ways to maintain relationships with said parties, even after marriage, but everyone must work to be a part of the solution, and that is something that must always be encouraged. For believers who may feel conflicted on the concept, the Bible did encourage "man to leave his parents and become one with his wife." This is a perfect example of just how sanctioned it is by the Bible. That is, marriage trumps family. This should help to alleviate any guilt in the case of bad in-laws who do not respect the boundaries of marriages, instead wishing to run the marriage of their child.

While I provided some staples for signaling and preparing for the financial journey within your relationship, the following are some pitfalls or red flags that can signal imminent financial challenges in your relationship:

1. One of you is unwilling to open a bank account; imagine working for years and years, and there is no interest in opening a bank account. As long as you don't share the same sentiments, then you can have a discussion with your spouse on the root

reasons and come to an agreement. While trying to convince your spouse, be sure to be armed with facts about the benefits of having an account.

2. One of you is unwilling to have a joint account. This is tricky. While I say couples on their way to marriage and throughout their married life should have joint accounts, I would also, conversely, say exercise much discernment if you or your spouse are contemplating this from your first date or short courtship. There are no hard, straight rules, but at every step, be diligent.

3. Frequent job changing, depending on the reasons for changing jobs, may be a red flag. Try to encourage your partner to see the benefits of staying with one employer. Again, it depends on the reasons for leaving as well. At any stage, with balanced and realistic deliberations, you or your spouse may just be better suited for any stop on the entrepreneurial spectrum, freelancing, microbusiness, or owning large businesses.

4. Financial infidelity is when there is no transparency in how the money is spent in the relationship or the agreed way of spending the money is not being adhered to consistently.

5. Spending more than you are earning is a red flag. In this case, I am not referring to one-time, occasional splurges that were saved for. I refer to consistent and total disregard for a budget, despite even having one. Red flag.

6. A poor credit rating is a red flag too if the rating is consistently poor without any effort to improve. This refers to credit abuse.

7. One of you is always unavailable to discuss finance, whether to plan or to address challenges with the finances in the relationship. This is another red flag. Consistent unavailability reflects a lack of commitment to the financial aspect of the relationship. Bills won't magically sort themselves, and debts won't magically pay themselves. It takes commitment and discipline.

8. Almost always borrowing consistently, both formally and informally, from families, friends, or loan shops is another red flag.
9. Only buying high-end brands in everything, regardless of affordability, or lack thereof, should be discouraged. Make every effort to remedy this habit. If your partner is unresponsive, then, like with any other red flag, be warned.
10. Not listening to your partner, especially on the topic of finances, is reckless and dangerous but specifically for those among us who believe that finances are too hard and complicated for women. Be guided by proven good judgment.

All these factors impact the financial bottom line in a relationship, for better or worse. Be guided accordingly, and always be willing to be flexible.

11. AM I MORALLY READY FOR A RELATIONSHIP?

Before you can answer this question truthfully, you must understand what morals are. No one on earth is qualified to fully judge morals; instead, they are a guide and set of agreed-upon precepts that then guide the behavior of a society. We also must take in the context of different cultures and respect the same.

Morals in this context are a system of beliefs, values, and principles of conduct, that as a world, we must first all agree on. Clearly that is not happening anytime soon. Morality is not a destination; it is, however, something one continuously works on. For instance, it is not something that will magically come to you when you reach a certain age, without putting in the work.

Understandably, morals are usually imprinted on a child at an early age. They form a great influence on their impressionable minds. The most basic way to do so is teaching the difference between right and wrong and fairness and unfairness. Conversely, what is evident is that children do not develop morals by what is verbally transferred to them but through assessing adults' actions with their direct and straightforward way of thinking, making parents the ones to hold their children accountable for their actions, regardless of what they were taught.

Being morally ready for a relationship means admitting where you are and assessing yourself based on your own personal values and beliefs. At its core, a relationship, especially biblically, requires a great level of character, humility, and sense of self. You can understand why morals are required to make a relationship last, and it requires morals from both partners. This means both partners should have the cognitive ability to have respect for their partners as well as to nurture a sense of purpose. This is specifically for those relationships that wish to transition to marriage.

Morality is formed much like how habits are formed. Continuous revisiting of beliefs creates a pattern, and if nothing else, your brain is a tool of habit. Compatibility is required in terms of morals, as otherwise, there will simply be a constant clash, brought on by differences in the makeup of each person. It can be anything simple from right versus wrong to more complex concepts. Basically, ideally, morals should be the blueprint of your daily actions, thoughts, words, and so on. Otherwise, it is just a theory that you hold. When morality means care, it means that everything you know and do will be employed in making you and your partner happy and comfortable.

Because all humans were created by God knowing good from bad and right from wrong, it is up to everyone to conduct him- or herself in a like manner. Morality should not be exercised occasionally in the relationship or when it suits one partner, especially in a heated argument. In such instances, morality could be used to deescalate these situations in your relationships; it requires patience and sometimes making sacrifices. Morality prevents relationships rife with pain and suffering caused to partners by each other. Morality teaches you to be sensitive to your partner's needs and wants but also to what causes him or her pain and discomfort.

Opportunities for morals are jealousy, dishonesty, infidelity of any kind, lack of care, respect, and decency. All of these have grave ramifications in a relationship and undoubtedly are shaped by one's morals or lack thereof. Your actions, I repeat, are a part of your morals, and you are responsible for them, unless you are declared mentally incapacitated. Your spouse is watching.

Jealousy is a common manifestation of lack of morals in a relationship, by either partner. Not only is it a signal of lack of trust, for a myriad of reasons, but it also can translate to discomfort, anxiety, and sadness in your partner if left unaddressed, whether its grounds are unfounded or not. Still using the "green-eyed demon" example, both partners have their roles in deescalating this situation, especially if it is baseless. If there is evidence of infidelity and there is no common ground, then I recommend mediation.

Dishonesty, in its purest form, is refusing to tell the truth for whatever reason, and depending on how much each partner may have invested in the relationship, realistically and in his or her mind, that may impact a partner's habit of refusing to tell the truth. Discernment can be a lifesaver, and partners should address all instances of dishonesty and take actionable steps to discontinue or curb the habit.

Conversely, telling the truth is never easy, but it is always the easiest way to ensure your partner suffers less physically, emotionally, and even financially because of your dishonesty. And when I say the truth, I mean the full truth, not just the amount you believe would placate your partner but even the details that he or she would not know to ask or think about. Put yourself in your partner's shoes Yes, it is after the fact, but there is still an opportunity to do the moral thing, as well as respect your partner's wishes after you have shared the truth, because truth be told, your partner may not like or receive the information well. But again, put yourself in your partner's shoes, and be reasonable.

Dishonesty is when, despite there being "communication," it was not truthful and so things like infidelity usually ensue. The road of infidelity holds nothing pretty, and true healing must take place as early as possible. Infidelity is another common example of immorality, affecting thousands of couples. Lack of communication plays a role in these scenarios. Infidelity signals a negative rebuke on your partner's morality. The fact remains that it is a signal of immorality and breaking of a truce, resulting in infidelity. Immorality is selfish, as the truth is no one would want his or her partner to cheat, and yet it happens. Again, immorality is doing unto others what you wouldn't want them to do unto you.

Lack of trust, or trust eroded by dishonesty, is among the hardest to rebuild. It could rock the very foundation of a relationship if left unaddressed and unattended. There is a saying that love cannot exist without trust. It may not be true for all cases, but the idea has merit. I can tell you for sure that there can exist no romance without trust. Consider that, even before getting married. Trust is a security provided to your partner; yes, it is not just physical security. Wouldn't you want your partner to feel secure?

Lack of care for your partner's emotions and his or her emotional investment is the opposite of good moral standing. It creates its own problems and exacerbates external stresses. It is best to address these matters after one has had an opportunity to cool off, to not create a toxic cycle of repaying hurt with hurt. No healing can come from that scenario. Conversely, caring and respect, in its many forms, in a relationship helps a relationship to thrive.

Trust in a relationship complements the level of morality in your relationships. Trust means reliability and dependability, not just because of one's words but also one's actions. Trust precedes love because you can only love someone you trust. It is the sense of security that is born from trust that allows partners to thrive. Again, love cannot exist without trust. Consequently, lack of trust in any relationship is a symbol of its inevitable collapse unless an intervention is done for that relationship.

It is morals that raise the standards of relationships. Morality should be able to withstand intruders in your relationship, in the forms of friends, exes, families, and sometimes a bone of contention between you and your partner. Whatever the intruder, both partners should put an end to it.

Lack of caring and respect in a relationship causes moral readiness to be stagnant, as that is the symbol of insensitive emotions. This creates a problematic scenario further compounded if the receiving partner decides to respond with insensitivity. This eye-for-an-eye gridlock does not help your relationship, and the only resistance in the relationship should be against immorality.

Absence of care and respect in a relationship leaves room for only hatefulness, and no successful relationship can be built on hatefulness. Ephesians 4:32 (NKJV) declares "And be kind to one and other, tenderhearted, for giving one another, even as God in Christ forgive you." Forgiving one another should be inserted in our everyday relational activities as a stable to motivate good behavior within the relationship. Care and respect speak volumes about one's moral integrity and that sense of security in your partner that was mentioned. Let it not be a case where you treat pets better than humans, especially humans you are pursuing a relationship with.

Morals also guide the default way you relate to and communicate with your partner. It pays to be kind, soft-spoken, and genuine. Being rude and inconsiderate achieves nothing positive for your relationship. Consider that it also does nothing positive for your morals. Your attitude and actions toward your relationship, especially rudeness, dishonesty, and inconsideration, only breed great levels of uncertainty. James 1:8 (NKJV) says, "He is a double-minded man, unstable in all his ways." The good news, however, is that your mind can be refocused, and once you are invested, you can know what it feels like to focus on your partner, in healthy and positive ways.

For believers, the Bible is a fertile teaching ground for many lessons, one of which, unsurprisingly, is morality. Here's a reminder why this journey must first be personal or individual before it can be collective. First Corinthians 15:33 declares, "Don't be deceived; evil company corrupts good habits." In context, this means relationships, whether platonic or romantic, can have that impact on someone's character. Your definition of morals must be in sync with your partner's, and again, it can be simple and basic like right or wrong; without this agreement, the relationship is disadvantaged from day one.

Galatians 5:19–21 (NKJV) gets more specific on the concept of morality declares, "Now the works of the flesh are evident, which are adultery, sorcery, hatred, contentiousness, jealousies, dissensions, heresies, envy, murders, drunkenness, revelries" and the like; in which I tell you beforehand, just as I also told you in time past, that those who practice such things will not inherit the kingdom of God." Attitudes and practices such as these are the enemy of moral character and signal the partner's lack of commitment to the moral compass of the relationship.

If you have any outbursts of wrath or violent expressions while you are feeling dissatisfied and angry with your partner, the situation needs to be defused as quickly as possible. Morality doesn't stop at thoughts; it extends to your ability to be conscious of said thoughts at any time, as well as your subsequent actions and reactions.

Make no mistake, morale and its development are years in the making and again are fed by what you are constantly exposed to. Plus, working on your morale means it must be something you value as an individual and thus would serve as an impetus for your efforts. Make no mistake, any efforts you have and ideals you hold, though admirable, can be tested by anyone, especially those closest to you. I have always wondered why that is so. Those closest to you may say and do things that would make you want to just put down your moral pursuits, just for a day at least, and react without consequences. Just expect this. I call it a moral battle, when what you know and hold of esteem is not what you want to do right away. Let's say your partner upsets you. Would your morals allow you to feel justified in denying him or her sex, refusing to administer his or her medication or cook his or her dinner, taking intimate details of the relationship outside, or rekindling a relationship with your ex? All are examples of what ideals being opposite actions would look like. Regardless, it sounds cliché, but in every unsavory situation, there is a potential for a good outcome.

Asking if you are morally mature or ready for a relationship is not just about how others assess you but also how you assess yourself, especially when no one is around to hold you accountable. Are you proud of yourself when there is no one around? You should assess everything from your unshared thoughts and intentions to your follow-up actions, which are clear to you whether you admit it or not, and seek opportunities to do better and thus to be better. It takes morality to stand up for what you believe in, to be someone who is empathetic, courageous, honest, and loyal and has fortitude, to name a few virtues.

Morality is when your words and actions are in one accord. Your deeds should be flawless, matching values. Your intentions should be positive and authentic. Morality is evident and should apply to all areas of one's life: religion, politics, and every human interaction in between, from running the red light to refusing to help a senior citizen cross a street and everything in between. The world as we see it is Exhibit A of what absence of morality within relationships can look like and the ripple effects it has.

Be in moral good standing and be diligent just as Romans 7:21 (NKJV) describes: "I find then a law, that when I would do good, evil is present with me." This speaks to the continuous valiant and present-minded effort it takes to establish and maintain one's own morals. Even if you catch yourself before making a move you deem wrong, the fact that it was your first reaction means that there is still work to be done but be encouraged.

Finally, morality is not an abstract concept or one for only a set amount of people or type of people, and just to be honest, the older one is the more invested one may have to be in order to achieve one's sought-after ideal morale.

On the subject of immorality, which takes many forms, I pause the regular proceedings to input a perfect example of lack of morality in the senseless killing of George Floyd on May 25, 2020, where he was sought by the Minneapolis police for use of a counterfeit twenty-dollar bill. How he died was where the grave immorality was displayed, because while his hands were handcuffed behind his back, a police officer knelt into his neck. He desperately tried to communicate that he couldn't breathe. It was when he realized his police abuser would not relent that he cried for his mother before giving up his ghost. That displays immorality on multiple levels.

In closing, relationships are inevitable in our society, and it is imperative that we all take some responsibility for nurturing the next generation and creating desirable ideals. Being morally ready for relationships can be difficult to maintain because of the basis of human existence, which guarantees both good and bad. Morality should be taught as early as the teenage years when humans are old enough to have developed a sense of self and knowledge of the cons and questions. Being taught this early has a direct relation to those values taking root and being habits of theirs as adults. It is never too late to learn morals, but let's just be honest: it is harder and less likely to stick with grown adults. This is one of those instances where it is evident the role that families have in our societies.

It is not too late for families now to change a generation and give future relationships an opportunity to surpass some of the current hindrances due to immorality.

12. AM I EMOTIONALLY READY FOR A RELATIONSHIP?

So far, I have taken you on a journey that explores the multifaceted experience that is uniquely human, and all this is for little benefit if you are not emotionally ready for a relationship. Again, the concepts are intertwined, and you can see them as you go about your day-to-day life. For example, despite your ideals and morals, if you lack the capacity to balance your emotive responses and actions, then again, it could be for naught.

If you consider nothing else before entering a relationship, you should always consider emotions. Because of the complexity of human interactions, one's emotions would be the center of that relationship.

As long as a person is still breathing, emotions are diverse and constantly changing, and that is why this quest takes constant effort. Emotions are the manifestations of our feelings, like hatred, anger, sadness, disgust, fear, pride, surprise, shame, excitement, happiness, and the most talked about, love. It would help though for parents to raise their children in a way that grooms their ability to manage their emotions. This would lead to more sustainable relationships.

Emotions are part of the package from the time we are born. Simply put, the concept of feeling is wired into our brains. Not everyone will feel the same way about the same thing, but all are born with the capacity to feel and relate to the concept of feeling. Again, exposure plays a great role in the frequency of any and all our feelings being triggered. It is also a fact that the richest soil to cultivate anything in a human being is during their childhood years. That is doubly so for emotions being elicited. This then means certain actions, whether accompanied or preceded by words, will elicit certain emotional responses. Again, some amount of this trigger response is taught, as a child not only checks his or her first reaction but also tests the waters to see what will be accepted, tolerated, praised, or lost. It is why I emphasize that families are the very fabric of societies and worlds because parenting is what hones a human being.

Now, with the 4-1-1 on emotions, you can understand why you would need to honestly assess your readiness for a relationship by this measure. Emotional maturity and stability are two ways in which you can assess yourself without being unkind to yourself. Here is how I try to navigate this topic without alienating or invalidating any relationship; it is by focusing on the goal. Be honest about how you feel, and you then can have a conversation with your partner and proceed from there. Be honest, open, and willing to accept feedback.

Relationships across the globe are confusing because of lack of emotional restraint being exercised, coupled with the lack of poise and emotional stability.

Emotional stability and maturity would seek to diffuse conflict and harsh, hurtful words and actions in a relationship, if that is not their goal. A couple should know what their goals are, on every level of the relationship, and the standards that they will uphold as a couple. Anything can be loud, chaotic, and confusing, with absolutely no focus. No one wants to be in a relationship where it sounds more like a football match than a relationship.

For believers who lean on the Bible for guidance, especially on an unscientific, in some ways, topic, I offer Galatians 5:22–23 (NKJV) as a good starting point. It speaks about self-control, which is basically the mastering of emotions. Paul is saying in part that we need to control ourselves. Self-control means we do not let our decisions spiral out of control because of a lack of control of our emotions. Self-control is a discipline that spiritually grows in us, but we must choose to deny our flesh and instead live in divine order.

Proverbs 25:28 (NKJV) declares that "He that hath no rule over his own spirit is like a city broken down and without walls." Essentially, self-control is the foundation of emotional maturity. A person who lacks self-control has less chance of sustaining a long-term committed relationship. This process is not just for introspection but also for an open and honest relationship, I always encourage these, no matter the topic.

Emotional maturity, depending on where you fall on the spectrum, can be any item on a SWOT table: strength, weakness, opportunity, or threat. You need to know as soon as possible, as the future of your relationship relies on it. Interestingly, engaging your emotions or seeking to take control of them involves exercising your mind. It takes a deliberate retraining of your thoughts and cognitive habits to better school your emotions. I implore those in singledom to spend the time to work on themselves and be better versions simply because they can. Their future relationship with a like-minded individual will thank them for it.

Lack of self-control is exemplified in so many ways and sometimes is used to deter further detriments in a relationship. Self-control sometimes translates to life opportunities that cannot be regained. Emotions could be managed deliberately to avoid unnecessary challenges. Lack of self-control can quickly spiral into self-destructive behaviors, going back to bad exes and poor practices unless you are able and willing to identify the gaps in the relationship where emotional immaturity is concerned. In instances like these, it will always lead to confusion. There can be no progress in a relationship in a state of confusion.

To have a backdrop of emotions is to take an introductory course in psychology. That is the purpose of education and edification, to better oneself, even if it is ultimately a career path one wishes to take. Education is obtained from material gathered on any topic, for individuals everywhere, on a shared concern or experience.

For example, before purchasing our first home, my wife and I sought to edify ourselves in publications on first-home ownership, and years later, we are thankful for it. We applied what we learned as we saved on time and money. Relationships are just the same, where one must do one's due diligence and always say, "Prevention is better than cure."

This is how I want all my readers to see preparing and assessing themselves for a relationship, as a journey of self-edification and applying what you have learned in your present or hopeful relationship to reap the rewards and benefits. Do not shy away from the work that may be put before you to work on yourself, your partner, and your relationship.

Being emotionally mature means being able to call out your own personal biases as what they are. And always remember to have an open mind. Another rule of thumb is to delay almost all decisions if you are incensed or overcome greatly by any emotion, meaning if you don't feel fully in control of your emotions and subsequent actions, that may not be the best time to make certain decisions without any supporting facts. You must also be open to your own perception and biases in said perceptions, which is the result of chemicals released in the brain, your belief system, and your brain's cognitive habits.

I'll go a step further to say that emotional instability is almost always evident, and once you see a trend of emotional instability, I urge you to proceed with caution. Your emotional readiness can be hindered by the choices you make, the actions you take, and the perceptions you gather in between. All of this is greatly influenced by emotions, and it can be an emotion that you feel in each moment. Therefore, mindset must be managed, and change is encouraged if needs be, as mindsets are easily affected by one's emotional state.

For you and your partner, here are a few components that can influence the manifestation of one's emotional state: your financial, moral, physical, and mental capacity. All around, there is a positive correlation between a healthy body, healthy mind, and healthy emotions. Emotions are sensory information, and one's mental capacity can help in processing and controlling that information.

Perception of your partner's emotions in a relationship can be swayed based on emotional maturity, and decisions are made in that split moment. There is importance in maintaining a balance, in managing one's emotions and the decisions made as a result. Because of the perplexity of human emotions and their ability to fake authenticity, it should be of great concern to every potential spouse to not overlook one's emotional status.

There is a direct link between mental and emotional health. Mental health has to do with one's capacity to process information, whereas emotional health refers to the ability to process emotions, which includes control. Your mental and emotional health are intertwined, not completely separated.

The formula goes a little something like, the physically healthier you are, the better chance you have at achieving mental wellness and vice versa. There is no escaping the interconnectedness between the mind and the body. Both factors affect the health of your emotions and your emotional responses.

Consider any ill-health as a possible complication for any event you may have in your relationship. Every aspect of who you are as a person, who your partner is as a person, and the type of relationship you have will have a direct and indirect impact on your emotions. It is one of the reasons I encourage people, wherever possible, to seek out compatibility, and that is not something that anyone else is more qualified to do then you and your partner. You can value advice from your inner circle, but ultimately, it is both of you who must admit what is happening in the relationship first.

As promised, here are a few indications of emotional immaturity:

1. Irritability—if you get irritated easily, easily cast blame on your partner, or take a long time to cool off and regain focus on the matter at hand, there may be a concern. Irritability can arise for a few reasons, and a few of them may be because of the existing relationship, including the uncertainty of said relationship. That in and of itself is a matter that also needs to be addressed, and it saves everyone's time to be honest, upfront, and present, always. Say, for instance, you don't feel as though either of you has gotten over your ex, it would be a good idea to be upfront as soon as possible and take a step back if needs be.

When you are not sure what you want out of life, this is a sign of immaturity. Uncertainty and unpredictability are the enemies of a good relationship.

2. Dishonesty—I would have explained in detail, in previous chapters, just how impactful the concept of honesty is and, even more so, the lack of it. If you or your partner are even initially tempted to be dishonest for any reason, it is a sign of immaturity, which means your relationship would be at further disadvantage.

An emotionally mature and ready person in contrast

1. Has a strong desire for a connection. The type of connection the person desires will be evident from as soon as you get past the niceties. Desire is what propels the person from just a concept in their minds to action. Desire is the vehicle that moves his or her fantasies forward, and this is not just in relationships but in general. Those who have a strong desire for something or someone do not consider failing any more than they have calculated, and interestingly, they will have an impressive success rate.

Your approach to life will determine if you succeed or fail. Even though life is filled with success and failure, you can chart the course of success only if you are determined amid the obstacles. Desire is like a road map: it gives you direction to get to the finish line.

2. Tolerance—yes, I have said it before and will say it again but probably in a different way. Temperament, humility, tolerance, and patience—all this means that how you communicate accepting or not accepting something or someone, is through tolerance. Tolerance is the talent to say that there are certain limits that you have, and you lovingly ask your partner to respect them, even if you both don't agree. Even if you agree to disagree with your partner, tolerance is the vehicle that should move that conversation.

Tolerance should translate to acceptance and not censoring. This is assuming that you and your partner have decided what matters most to you in a relationship and what your limits are as a couple. Suffice it to say, to a certain extent, there should be some tolerance of your partner's perceived imperfections, considering how they impact your relationship. You show tolerance while you and your partner work on these imperfections, as your partner should not be worried about being themselves completely around you.

3. One's ability to acknowledge a potential for conflict or contention and resist the urge to contend—basically, this means not fighting fire with fire. It means being able to walk away in the height of tension with an expressed intent to revisit at a time when tensions or heightened emotions don't prevent a resolution or agreement in handling the problem at hand.

Conflicts in relationships, to an extent, are unavoidable, and with that said, one should not fear conflict. Emotional readiness and maturity will eradicate that fear for you, once you have a working appreciation of how conflicts should be handled to also ensure resolution, preferably without repeating said conflict. If viewed and addressed properly, conflicts can serve as a rich learning tool for couples, and before long, said conflicts will happen less and less often.

4. Having no interest in dating multiple partners while being in a monogamous relationship—it was inevitable to mention, and here it is. Once you aim to find yourself a suited partner, meaning one person, then giving up multiple dating partners should be a celebration of growth and you finding what you sought. It shows transformation and maturity, as one focuses on commitment and devotion.

Changing from multiple partners to one partner is a sign of emotional and moral readiness. It also signals a transition from dating to courting. Dating one partner also speaks volumes to maturity and your level of commitment and dedication to one person. Being devoted to one person in a relationship speaks to communication and respect for both one's partner and the potential of the invested relationship.

5. Leaving your ex, after you have left them—you heard me. It is more common than you think to fixate on your ex. Quite frankly, people do need some time to move on from their exes and learn all they can from that relationship and its fateful ending. Also interesting is that some go back to their exes because of things left unsaid, issues left unresolved, and either partner not being satisfied with the lack of closure.

Ideally, do not enter another relationship with unresolved issues with your soon-to-be-ex, though that is not how it is marketed nowadays. Ignore the noise. Depending on how intense the relationship was, or the breakup even, it may guide you on how much tact and purposefulness you would have to exercise in your next relationship, so that you no longer relive the past or want to. Plus, to your next partner, it should not be where the ghost of your ex haunts your new relationship and has any impact whatsoever, but that is ideal. Reality requires constant hard work.

6. Mastering the art of communication—the heartbeat of every relationship is communication. But there are a few things before speaking words, which by the way is not the only way to communicate. You must be purposeful with your communication. What emotion do you want to evoke in your partner, what point do you want to convey, and what response are you expecting? Your partner would greatly like this, plus as much information as possible, and, yes, this is particularly so for heart-to-heart conversations.

Emotional readiness impacts how you communicate because emotions impact your thoughts. If you are feeling defensive, you may just communicate only information that would seek to absolve you from any guilt, instead of deciding why you need to communicate what you want to communicate. That is unfair to your partner, who cannot read minds, despite the added tidbits that body language may give. Every emotion affects your senses and how you retain information, this how you relay it. Now you see why it is important to keep said emotions in check. But you must admit them before you can control them.

7. The ability to compromise—there is no emotional readiness without compromise, simply because things will never be how you want them, all the time. Compromise is just a fancy way, in some instances, of saying that you need to always consider your partner's feelings. Also, compromise is deciding what is more important, you sticking to your ways, especially at your partner's inconvenience, or both of you agreeing on middle ground? Think about it. Compromise also doubly serves to indicate that you are empathetic to your partner and his or her needs, not just your ways. No matter how long you are with your spouse, it is not constant yet constantly required, as humans evolve.

Relationships on a whole thrive on compromises and negotiations. Even being married for thirty-three years, my wife and I still have great appreciation for the importance of compromise. Lack of compromise is like stretching a rubber band to its limits, only for it to regain form. This speaks to resistance, and in relationships, human interactions on a whole, the less resistance, the better.

8. Saying goodbye to your relationship checklist—for some, it works, and so I wouldn't seek to discredit it. For some, checklists are long and can get very specific. The only thing I caution is to prioritize said list. It shows emotional maturity to grasp that you may not get everything you want, but you would have assessed necessities as opposed to wants in your relationship.

Once the checklist has served its purpose, there is nothing wrong with retiring said list. Checklists are to ensure consistency and completeness in certain tasks and objectives; once these are achieved, so too can the checklist be obsolete, having served its purpose. When you naturally feel as though you have no need for the checklist, you have autonomously become mature and ready.

9. Another one: self-control—yes, I say it again, because every bit of progress can be unraveled in a moment of loss of self-control. Self-control is a marker of emotional stability, which is ironic since emotions are known to change depending on various impacting factors. But nonetheless, self-control is the ability to have a handle on said emotions and responses at any given moment, especially in clearly difficult situations.

Self-control is the ability to control oneself, one's emotions and desires, or the expression of one's behavior, especially in difficult situations. Again, I implore parents to recognize the opportunity. They must mold humans with moral values embedded and an ingrained sense of self-control that can prevent ills and practices such as addictions, substance abuse, and so on.

I do believe each trait speaks for itself about how vital and practical it would be in a relationship. I hope they provide some value to you, as I share what I would have done for the better part of thirty years, as well as what I witnessed and have counseled others on during my time in the ministry.

Getting to the finish line of emotional readiness takes a lot of dedication, self-discipline, and determination. It takes determination that will ultimately lead to success. This success should be weighed by equal amounts of innate ability, motivation, and personal goals within a relationship. Monitoring one's own progress helps one to stay focused and possibly deter against temptations. Because emotional readiness is not an inherent skill, the work is worth it. It will save your relationship and your sanity.

Remember, a relationship, marriage, is not a destination. It is an important flagpole on your journey in this race called life.

13. DIGNITY PRESERVATION IN A RELATIONSHIP

The beginning and ending of a well-deserved relationship hinge on dignity preservation. The challenge to cultivating this concept comes from distractions, based on our environments and cultures, that are constantly changing, especially with the advent of current and emerging technologies. I have learned that we must be adaptable when facing change, and the path to preserving dignity in a relationship must be approached in the same way. If we, however, choose to remain complacent, we will be left behind to suffer the consequences, and our relationships will suffer too. The reality remains that too many people turn to relationships with no idea what they are looking for, what they are willing to accept, or what they are ready to give to that relationship. They do not even think about the importance of the dignity of a relationship and how it will affect the relationship positively or negatively.

May I say that dignity is the right of a person to be valued and respected for his or her own sake and to be treated equally and ethically. It is your inalienable right to demand respect and honor in all causes; thus, the act of dignity should be given the highest priority in any relationship. Dignity should serve as a benchmark to fortify and stabilize every action being displayed in a relationship. Establishing a marker, a standard of dignity in your relationship, will help to alleviate current or developing problems. It would also assist you in keeping your eyes under the hood for any indicator of possible engine failure during your journey.

WHAT IS THE MEANING OF DIGNITY IN A RELATIONSHIP?

Dignity is the measuring rod of how you allow yourself to be treated by your partner in a relational partnership and, in turn, how you treat your partner. Dignity, or the lack thereof, can dictate if you accept cheating, lying, abuse, and neglect from your partner—if you allow yourself to be treated like a sex object or a walking time bomb, humanly speaking. You own whatever you accept in your life, and that is where dignity comes in. You can either qualify or rule yourself out from being dignified, but it does not excuse or justify undignified behavior. Often, one disqualifies oneself simply by one's own actions, all the while portraying oneself as dignified. You cannot preach one thing but live the complete opposite, waiting for or expecting credit from your partner.

Michael J. Fox said, "One's dignity may be assaulted, vandalized, and cruelly mocked, but it can never be taken away unless it is surrendered." Surrendering speaks of ceasing resistance to your enemy, opponent, or partner and submission to his or her authority. In this context, the only sure way that your dignity can and will be taken away is if you submit your will to your own partner. Your will is your prized treasure and should not be broken or exchanged for personal gains or temporary pleasures. For example, you should not say yes to every excited promise of your partner. All that ends up with no bottom. It would be better to ensure the promise is authentic prior to saying yes or being emotionally invested.

Here are instances where people who said yes traded their dignity for cheap returns:

1. People judge potential partners to be more, when in fact they were not who they portrayed themselves to be. You are being judged on the merit of your attire and your speech during dating. Judging is to form an opinion or a conclusion on someone. Logically speaking, you cannot form a correct opinion about an individual you have met only once. In a court setting, before a judge rules or passes a verdict, he or she must hear and receive evidence from both the plaintiff and defender. Likewise, if someone tells you that he or she drives a tractor trailer, unless that person showed you a commercial driver's license (CDL), you should not believe him or her unquestioningly. This is a basic and realistic example.

2. Some forfeit all their principles, values, and morals to sleep with someone to initiate a relationship. This one is a no-brainer. Redirecting or ignoring your spiritual values and convictions to please someone is baseless, cheap, and insensitive, and moreover, it doesn't help the potential of a relationship. Harnessing your dignity or bringing it under control speaks volumes and is a marker for admirable self-achievement. It should be complimented. It shows courage and motivates those who are looking up to you for direction and answers to their struggles with their weaknesses. Self-dignity goes a far way in one's relationship.

3. Acceptance of humiliation and degradation during a discussion sends the wrong signal to the one who gave it. Someone verbally and emotionally demeaning you should not be tolerated publicly or privately. Ignorance is the lowest form of humiliation and suffering. It is not just the pain and the wounds inflicted; the humiliation lingers longer than any physical wounds, which can heal. It is not so much how it was said but what was said that could make something much more painful. People do to you,

but you allow them to do so, especially the second time around. Some people will only love you as much as they can use you. Their loyalty ends where the benefits stop.

4. Promises and betrayal can be wrapped into a ball of confusion, from promising a Rolls-Royce to getting married. In fact, the individuals in question do not even have a job when the subject matter is investigated. Betrayal happens with both males and females, but for the most part, it happens to females more frequently. Betrayal can end up being fatal if taken to heart. Imagine a situation where you grew up in a home with high moral standards, had a great job, and were highly educated, leaving all your achievements and morality to live with a nonworking man. Emotional infidelity is far more damaging to a relationship than sexual infidelity. Lies are the ultimate betrayal in a relationship.

Advantages of dignity in a relationship cannot be overstated enough because your dignity is not your market worth but your natural worth, and this is priceless. Humanly speaking, priceless items are being cared for because of their inherent worth. For example, you may prefer wearing your old boots in twelve-inch deep snow rather than your new ones. Likewise, your partner should be looked at as your priceless treasure in life, and conversely, you should feel so treasured. You would not want to say or do anything to make him or her feel rejected and worthless but rather to choose your words before you speak. Even your tone should be polite and calm. Whatever you are doing, it should be done for your partner's advantage.

Your dignity makes kindness to yourself and others easier by giving you perspective on your natural limits. You should first own and control dignity before you can impact someone else's life by your example and your actions; your determination to maintain your point of view and passion for dignity in a relationship can allow for a healthy challenge for the people in your circle to also pursue dignity in their relationships. Let us look at this concept as being magnetic with the ability and capacity to literally transform the status quo in relational incompetence.

Dignity is not unique to you; it is shared by all, and it does not allow you to be prejudiced in favor of one person over another in a way considered to be unfair. This concept creates a platform or forum to accommodate honest discussions of the idea of achieving and managing personal dignity in a relationship. It would reflect harmony and agreement despite being biased. Bias should not be looked at as a negative occurrence in a relationship, especially if both partners understand each other. Being biased occasionally may spark healthy conversations that will subsequently help you form a good opinion about each other, thus enhancing and adding more value to the relationship. It is called *compromise* and is not undignified once base values remain intact for each partner.

Your dignity also informs your talents and abilities; it puts you in touch with your natural gifts rather than the expectations of others. Everyone was born with some degree of talent, but it was given to us based upon our natural abilities. For example, either partner in a relationship can possess the ability to master public speaking, which can direct a relationship's attention to the ministry. This, of course, calls for honesty and high moral standing, because one person was transformed into a preacher. Subsequently, his wife would see the need to be adaptable into a similar personality of a preacher. This is dignity transformation and emulating a relationship.

In my earlier years of growing up, I had zero dignity. The influence of friends misleading me to do bad things was always there. Transitioning from teenager years to adulthood was much more difficult for me to embrace, since the distractions of the opposite sex and going to parties were profound. Nevertheless, dignity showed up in my life the very moment I was called to ministry. I began to see life differently than before. My thought processes changed immediately. I had to wonder if I was living in the same world after my eyes were opened. It is unexplainable how swiftly one's mind can switch from bad to good and from wrong to right. It is like I was having a nightmare.

In the process of time, after I had decided to fully surrender my life to the Lord, many of my friends gave me days, weeks, months, and even a few years before I returned to my old path and ways. I have proven them all wrong, even though it was not easy to maintain that which I have started. There was a time when I thought my newfound and claimed dignity was too difficult to possess and maintain. The reason it was difficult was because I was not depending on a higher power; instead, I was relying on my own strength, which translated to failure by default. Then one day, while reading the Bible, I came across this scripture: "I can do all things through Christ who strengthens me" (Philippians 4:13 NKJV). This, of course, was the beginning of an awakening for me, but I never stopped believing in that word. Fast-forward, I was supernaturally called to be a pastor and preacher, which placed much more pressure on my life to understand and live a dignified life before my family and fellow men. Of course, it does not make me perfect, but this awakening continues to enhance my spiritual relationship with the eternal one and deepens my relationship with Him.

As for my wife, my transformation and transition into the ministry has placed enormous pressure on her mind, body, soul, and spirit. She had no problem being called a sister in the Lord but never imagined before being called first lady; however, it keeps both of us in the corridor of righteousness, always walking on thin lines because we know who we are and whose we are. Dignity can change one's perspective.

WHAT CONSTITUTES DIGNITY IN A RELATIONSHIP?

There are several components to the recipe for authentic dignity in relationships. If both partners understand the purpose and functionality of dignity and then utilize it appropriately, dignity will not be a thing of the past but rather of the present and future for all relationships that embrace the concept and moral compass.

Here is a list of eleven elements of dignity:

1. Fairness
2. Independence
3. Safety
4. Inclusion
5. The benefits of doubt
6. Acceptance of identity
7. Recognition
8. Understanding
9. Acknowledgment
10. Accountability
11. Tolerance

1. FAIRNESS

It is almost a working relationship with one another. Both parties have a responsibility to recognize and respect their relationship's needs. It's about dreaming, having a shared vision for your relationship, and working hard toward its success. This is not to say by any means that either partner's needs are unimportant; they are important and should not be taken for granted. Equality should be transparent in the relationship and should be demonstrated at all costs for both partners. However, consideration should be given for the woman because she has been called the weaker vessel in the Bible.

In our modern society, the term "weaker vessel" is a thing of the past since most women are competing very vigorously with men in the working environment. They should be continuously encouraged to apply wisdom. Equality means that each partner's interests and desires are respected and met reasonably, as opposed to just one partner's needs dominating a relationship. In contrast, inequality in relationships refers to an imbalance of responsibility and power between partners. Anything that is an imbalance, sooner or later, becomes problematic; imagine it being like trying to run with one of your legs being amputated.

The principle of equality and fairness in relationships is a basic human right. The principle will only be effective when one is doing the right thing or right doing is carried out, consistently and without hesitation. As an adult, you know right from wrong and good from bad, as you were born with that conscientiousness. The problems start to arise when partners pretend to be in another world where nothing is wrong, instead of confronting the challenges in a relationship. Problems in the world began with the very people who lived in the world. Likewise, nothing is wrong with the relationship; the people who are in the relationship have issues that affect their partners.

The real meaning of fairness in a relationship is when both partners are constantly trying to outdo their partner in everything or in every area in their relationship. My wife and I have a unique understanding, a friendship, as it relates to doing chores in our home. When she is doing laundry, I am in the kitchen cooking; while she is doing the ironing, I am sweeping the floor. When she is folding the clothes, I am washing the dishes. This is what dignity, equality, and fairness look like. Unfairness is one party doing almost everything while the other party is watching TV. Neither partner should settle for this kind of behavior. Shared dignity would not allow for this.

2. INDEPENDENCE

Independence is when you are empowered to act on your own behalf as it relates to making good judgment calls, and it comes with the feeling that you are in control of your life and how you react to certain experiences, resulting in a sense of hope and possibility. It has to do with having leverage in your relationship to make decisions that will enhance your life and your relationship. Dignity is when you can feel good about yourself based on the choices you make and the decisions you execute independently. It's like looking in the mirror and giving yourself a pat on the back. Independence does not mean being rude and disrespectful to your partner but rather doing things that agree with the relationship, with values shared by both partners.

If you feel like spending time by yourself or with friends or family, you should not have to beg your partner for permission. On the contrary, your partner should not feel insecure and threatened by you exercising your independence. Independence is being able to afford yourself to an extent, without solely depending on your partner. Independence does help your self-esteem; it eliminates stress, forges a lot of moments, and allows you to live in a relaxed environment. It's advantageous being independent in a dignified relationship.

3. SAFETY

Safety is a predominant element in dignity. The definition is the quality or condition of being safe; freedom from danger, injury, or damage; or having security in the environment you have found yourself in, that is, being excluded from hazardous behavior that has the potential to interfere with your relationship. Safety puts people at ease in two ways. Psychological security is where they feel free of concerns about being embarrassed, humiliated, or ashamed for speaking up or for expressing their emotions, which they do without fear of retribution or rebuke. The other is physical security, where partners feel free from bodily harm and physical hurt. Safety is not an understatement but rather a prerequisite to dignity in a relationship, especially from a female's perspective. Females feel safe if they believe the relationship is on the path to success, by their personal definitions and even societal ones. In retrospect, lots of women were short-sighted or reluctant to get involved in relationships that never worked because of the constant abuse, mentally, physically, verbally, and even emotionally. Unfortunately, because no one was pursuing a dignified relationship, they would allow any kind of abuse or at least tolerate it. Let me interject and say, safety in a relationship is not 100 percent guaranteed all the time, because human beings are imperfect.

Safety, however, should be the highest priority in one's life, as every activity that you do daily has the potential to endanger some aspect of your life or the lives of others, both directly and indirectly. You need to safeguard your health first and then your dignity, which you would have spent long days and nights to establish. Your dignity in a relationship makes you credible in the eyes of your partner and even beyond those in your circle. Women need to feel a sense of emotional safety in the relationship by checking in with the level of the shared self-esteem in both partners. History shows that women with low self-esteem are more likely to fall prey to physical, emotional, and financial abuse, so women should safely guard their destiny.

4. INCLUSION

Inclusion is when each partner has a deep sense of belonging to one another. Without knowing the question being asked, suspicion lingers in one's mind; inclusion seeks to eradicate some of these suspicions. Possessing similar views and ideas regarding dignity will provoke both partners to show selfless appreciation toward one another. Positive views and ideas close the door for negative intruders and intentional distraction. Another viewpoint of inclusion is that it does not stop with both partners but goes into the family tree of both partners. There is a popular saying on the topic of inclusion, that when you marry a person, you marry his or her family; in many instances, this has proven to be true.

Family members being inclusive in your relationship has many advantages; it adds value to your relationship since the communication platform opens for both partners to know their in-laws personally and to establish mutual trust and friendship. Can you imagine your partner's family despising you or if they cannot stand your presence? What if whenever you are around, they feel threatened? On the contrary, having relationships with your in-laws creates influence and balance that can impact their curiosity toward pursuing a dignified lifestyle. Without a relationship, you are limited to establishing some of the most exciting moments in someone's life. Inclusion is all about coming together with the aim to be an agent of change.

In my own personal experiences, I believe that my lifestyle has had an indelible effect on most of my in-laws. They trust me purely, meaning to the full extent of being harmless to their trust. They feel comfortable with having me in their circle. For thirty-three years of marriage to their sister, aunt, or cousin, I have never received any negative vibes. The main purpose for me being a part of that family is to be the mediator to settle differences, when necessary. They listen to me, value my advice, and act accordingly. I am included in the intricacies of their family by marriage and by them seeking my advice.

5. THE BENEFIT OF THE DOUBT

This is to accept someone as honest and deserving of trust, even though there are or might be doubts or indicators that the person might be lying. You still must give him or her the benefit of the doubt initially and accept what he or she says for now, until unequivocally proven otherwise. The benefit of the doubt creates a platform for the conversation to be prolonged instead of being short-lived. The more you communicate, the more information will be gathered in the case of fact-finding about a certain incident that involves one or both partners. This will help in uncovering the truth. The benefit of the doubt should be given on the grounds of serious vetting and cannot identify any visible evidence that contradicts what was presented as truth. Act accordingly without malice.

You should treat everyone as being worthy, responsible, and accountable, starting with the premise that everyone has good motives and is acting with integrity. You are alleging that they are in their rights to do what they have done. There is an old phrase that was coined by the British barrister Sir William Garrow: "A person is innocent until proven guilty. If there is no evidence found after he was alleged as the suspect, you should give him the benefit of the doubt. If he, however, was found guilty of the act due to evidence found, then he should no longer be given the presumption of innocence."

6. ACCEPTANCE OF IDENTITY

This can have both negative and positive views, as it relates to dignity, especially in the context of the values of a relationship. There are several factors that guide this narrative that can make it complicated at times, depending on whom you ask, as the answer could be varied. Some folks are reluctant to accept other people if they are not introduced to them by a well-known personality or have not had a prior relationship with them. The truth is that everyone is walking around with some form of suspicion or opinion of his or her neighbor or even a stranger, who is no less an equal, fellow human being. This insecure attitude widens the span of unrealistic and callus rejections of one of the very core values of dignity and respect that exists for every human being, regardless of whether we chose to acknowledge it or not.

You should not overstate the naked facts: that acceptance of identity gives people the absolute freedom to express their authentic selves without reservation of being judged negatively and people should be able to interact without prejudice or having a sense of feeling like a lesser person. Also, we must accept how religion, gender, class, race, sexual orientation, and disability can be at the very center of their identities. Assume they have moral standing and a moral compass that are guided by their highest values and character. Remember, dignity cannot be hidden under a blanket; either you have it, or you do not.

Acceptance of identity should not be reneged upon, by virtue of one's disabilities, religion, or race, as I briefly stated in the previous paragraph. I am speaking, specifically and personally, for the speechless and the less fortunate in our society or on its fringes, who have been constantly rejected instead of being embraced by our society as the equals they are. It is a societal nightmare that reaches the souls of the so-called "nobody cares" population. Jesus taught us to love everyone. The Bible tells us that for this purpose, he came. Matthew 18:11 (NKJV) says, "For the son of man has come to save that which was lost." The expression of dignity is not a one-way street, and it's not to be done by only a certain class of people. It is being expressed in diverse ways with people from all walks of life. Let us help the helpless.

As you pay attention to the less fortunate ones, you are literally pulling them out of self-pity and pride to a place of capacity and influence, helping them realize their inherent roles as dignified human beings. Pride feeds our self-images and always comes before a fall, but dignity nourishes you in every area of your life, and for those seeking a relationship, you need this tool in the toolbox for making your relationship work. Dignity is not about our social status, achievements, or money; it's an expression of who you are, hence the reason why we should affirm ourselves and maintain self-compassion whether we experience failure or success. Our dignity should be built on a foundation of kindness, honesty, and authenticity. Pride promotes our superiority, but dignity is wrapped up with gratitude and humility.

7. RECOGNITION

In its simplest form, recognition is an acceptance of a claim as true or valid. For instance, people are selfish when it comes to their own recognition, as being someone deserving of a well-needed reward for their service, loyalty, truth, or even dignity. They assess themselves as being worthy of the recognition when in fact they may not deserve to be recognized by another's standards. The language of self-worth has literally plagued the minds and intentions of many believers and self-centered individuals. It's unfortunate that the game of worthiness is not realized in our culture to give us more leverage. Recognition should be the hallmark of influence and promote dignity to whoever is willing to embrace it.

Evidently, being recognized for the least efforts in whatever area of your life makes you have a feeling of self-worth. Telling people thanks for the contribution they share in your organization and reminding them that they are an asset to your organization's growth speaks volumes. Remarks of this magnitude immediately change the trajectory of an individual's own performance and will exponentially matriculate to the next level. *Recognition* is the magic word in many regards. If you want to see your partner grow exponentially, you must nurture him or her with the proper remarks, affirmations, admiration, and appreciation.

Dignity is and will always be the admission that we are worthy of better things and better relationships. You should never settle for undignified lifestyles. Walk with your head up and your chest squared, portraying healthy self-esteem and self-worth. Your self-worth and dignity should be provocative enough to influence your partner to come up higher, regarding his or her own recognition and practice of dignity. It will always be more productive to have solitude than a life with incomplete relationships. You should not lose your dignity while being subject to your partner's evident lies and deceptions. There is one thing that all liars have in common, and it is that they are controlling. They hide their feelings and are inherently insecure. For these reasons, they spread lies and rumors, and you risk your dignity for self-destruction.

8. UNDERSTANDING

Understanding is to exercise insight and good judgment to determine the level of dignity in a person's life. Every thriving relationship needs to maintain mutual respect and consistently so. Sometimes it takes quite a bit of explanation and pouring out of understanding before reconciliation can be achieved. Especially in a relationship, one needs to acknowledge one's limitations, poor judgment, and lack of insight to calm the flame of misunderstanding the quality of one's partner's dignity. Dignity does not exempt you from making a point to your partner or anyone when your dignity is being questioned.

Understand that it is not a coincidence that your dignity is being questioned or being misunderstood and that this is a perfect opportunity to make a formal presentation to the questioner as it relates to dignity. In cases of your dignity being questioned, you need to lay out to them, in no uncertain terms, that trying to understand one's dignity is different for everyone, because in part it hinges on an individual's personality. Personality is also expressed in diverse ways. Also, it is not just what a person does that defies his or her dignity but how and why he or she did it. I'll give you an example. If I am loud when being provoked, does that mean I do not have dignity? Absolutely and resoundingly, no. It simply means that I had my reasons for raising my voice.

9. ACKNOWLEDGMENT

Acknowledgment speaks of recognition of the importance and quality of one's dignity. Everyone who is making a difference in his or her lifestyles, hobbies, organizations, or even societies need to be put in the spotlight of recognition or acknowledgment. As I alluded to in previous paragraphs, giving someone, especially your partner, your undivided attention will help boost his or her courage positively to do much more than he or she is doing. Everyone who has achieved the pinnacle of his or her pursuit of dignity would like to showcase his or her success to friends and family.

If your dignity has been lost during your transition to a more serious relationship, you should admit this to your partner or ex-partner, especially if he or she was the main contributor to the loss. People should be held accountable and acknowledge the damage that their actions have dealt to your dignity. You could lose your dignity by the mere fact that your partner has lost his or her love for you and what you do when you find out. You have identified this because he or she keeps putting space and distance between you, and you suddenly find yourself chasing behind your partner because your love is still hot for him or her. If you have recognized that your partner has done something wrong and that he or she is upset with you, then you should not go insane after him or her. You should not be afraid to get tough with him or her. Chasing after your partner would subsequently and ultimately destroy your dignity.

Trying over and over to get someone to see things from a different perspective is self-defeating and, ultimately, insanity. Start over and begin that process by loving yourself. If you cannot respect yourself, why should anyone else respect you? It starts and ends with you. Acknowledgment in this context means that you need to give your partner your full attention by listening to, validating, and responding to his or her concerns and the pain and discomfort he or she has gone through. You must also be present in your own journey to achieving dignity to support your partner.

10. ACCOUNTABILITY

Accountability is an owner's own blameworthiness, liability, and expectation of account giving. Believe it or not, you will be held in high esteem or low esteem for your dignity. People in your circles, even your partner, will question your dignity, verbally or nonverbally, in private or in public. In those instances, what you say, what you do, is what holds you accountable to your own dignity. Also, who are you in a relationship when it comes to matters of accountability, in maintaining your standards, your dignity? I am not suggesting that you walk and live with your head bent low, as that certainly would not be the qualifying factor to determine the level of your dignity; however, every moment and opportunity counts. Do you consistently choose to ignore standards and dignity in yourself or your partner?

In retrospect, you should always be able to take responsibility for your own actions, especially if you have broken a promise or failed to comply with the dignified standards of another person—even more so if that person is your partner. Apologizing, for example, is an act of accountability as you are telling the person that you acknowledge your errors and faults that caused your dignity to be in peril or in pain. Taking this approach demonstrates some degree of responsibility and respect for you by your partner and fellow human beings. With this, people will begin to look at you differently and even begin to question your dignity less.

The next big step you need to consider is showcasing accountability in self-dignity as you make a commitment to be dedicated and change hurtful behaviors—those that are hurtful to yourself and to your fellow people. You can inflict mental and physical pain on others' lives by what you say to them or your attitude toward them. There is a wise saying "Who feels it, knows it." It is always wiser to invest in building someone up than to tear down someone. When you empower someone, that person in turn becomes a motivator for others and a force to reckon with, based on what you would have instilled in him or her. Certainly, we need everyone who is in a relationship to possess a high degree of dignity. Let's make it happen by first doing it and being it.

11. TOLERANCE

This is the capacity to endure continued subjection to something. In this context, it is perfect or imperfect dignity. To maintain your dignity in a culture that is constantly bombarded by diverse wickedness is challenging for the best among us. The fact that you cannot blindfold yourself or stick cotton in your ears to avoid seeing and hearing things that would dilute your dignity is just unfortunate.

You should condition your mind to understand that what you see or hear will affect your functions and how far your dignity will be tested. It has been proven since the beginning of time that the very best of us fail to completely maintain a life that is dignified, yielding to no temptation. Our perception is one thing that is the driving force behind most failures. Whatever our eyes behold, whatever good or bad, our minds capture it to repeat it by executing it. Remember that your mind is like a battlefield. Everything you see and hear is being transmitted to your mind. Your mind resembles a computer hard drive that stores all the data that it captures.

Your tolerance level will run high whenever your partner or the people in your circle maintain their dignity. In contrast, your tolerance level will run low when your partner and the people in your circle do not maintain their dignity. What is exciting to know in this scenario is there is no extreme either positively or negatively. There is a balance in the process. Sometimes you are feeling sick in your body, and sometimes you are feeling well; it is no different with dignity in your relationship or human dignity overall.

14. WHAT IS THE PATH TO PRESERVING DIGNITY IN RELATIONSHIPS?

All people pursuing a relationship should envision the beginning and the results that they are anticipating for themselves and their soon-to-be partners. I am suggesting having a vision for yourself and the person you wish to be with, long before you even meet in person. That way, you can have an idea when you do meet him or her. You have an idea what his or her values should reflect and so on. My best recommendation toward this world-class event is to treat it like you are preparing to embark on a remarkable adventure, because that is what it might be like. Human errors naturally occur when one is venturing into a matter of this magnitude, and you want to make as few mistakes as possible during and even after the process. So, the pathway is to commit every aspect of your intentions to memory like a mantra or even document them on a piece of paper. Do not try to be Superman in this venture, where you only have one weakness, kryptonite, but see it and visualize it as if your life depends on it. Your primary objective is to limit the public suspicion once and for all.

At the same time, depending on your age, you are minimizing the time and energy you spend, which you may need later when the dust settles.

Permit me to elaborate on the importance of putting together a written vision of an ideal partner prior to the actual relationship. The definition of *vision* is the ability to think about or plan with doses of imagination, reality, wisdom, knowledge, and understanding. A professional builder will demand a blueprint prior to beginning construction on any property, and no two blueprints are ever the same. The overarching idea is to have a plan. A blueprint is a design plan with other technical drawings showing the details and specification of the pathway of construction for a building. A vision is nothing less than the blueprint, so do not spare the details in your vision. It is what makes your vision undeniably yours. Your vision should spell out every intended detail of your adventure. The schedules should also be inserted, which, of course, will help you navigate every possible detail of your planned future.

Remember, success is inevitable through sacrifice and hard work. A mind that is focused, sober, committed, and meticulous is a mind that is unstoppable in its pursuit and its goals. Treat your relationship as one of those goals. The very first time I began to pursue my wife, my attitude was deliberate and focused; I knew exactly what I was looking for. I had prayed about it beforehand. I believed in myself and in my prayers, and in the process of time, my prayers were answered. What the Creator has done for others, He can do for you also.

WHY SELF PRESERVATION

Self-preservation is one of the most valuable gifts that we can give to ourselves. It is needed to some extent in preserving dignity in a relationship. We self-preserve by honoring our desires and needs, knowing our limits, and taking the time to develop our inner selves to fight against all possible intrusions on the self. Being committed to marshal the repair and healing of our own spirits from every form of evil is important to our well-being also and should not be taken lightly.

Importantly, it should form a part of our plan to live this life. The inner man enables you to give yourself much more energy to radiate your internal light. Naturally, understanding our limits in our daily activities should be a marker in guiding our capacity for preservation. Knowing your limits helps you avoid certain situations that would test your abilities adversely.

Self-preservation is the protection of oneself from hurt, danger, harm, and ultimately death. Every human being has the right to defend his or her existence from destructive and evil elements. Self-preservation says, "I will save and protect myself first before I can save and protect my partner or someone else." What if you and your partner both capsized in the ocean? Your first instinct will be to save yourself even if you must hold tight to the boat or something else. After that, you try to save your partner.

Self-preservation is also viewed as a universal, natural response of a living organism perceiving a threat upon its life. Every creature in respect to its size and exposure to danger will move away from a perceived threat, especially if it is impossible to manage or confront. Creatures will operate on their instincts by doing absolutely whatever is needed or possible at that moment to neutralize or minimize the threats on their life. This is no different than how a human being would operate in real time.

I have personally experienced and understood self-preservation in its simplest form. One of the most dramatic experiences I had was about twenty-six years ago, when I was attacked by two thugs with guns. On approaching my car with my six-month-old baby and my two-year-old daughter, suddenly there was a sensation coming from behind that signaled danger was at hand. It was time for me and my babies' preservation. I turned around, and the thugs were already in my face. One said, "Do not move."

I responded, "Why not?"

The next thing I knew, the gun went off, the baby fell from my arms, and my two-year-old daughter also fell. I should have mentioned that it was a cold, snowy evening. I became numb and was for a split second dumbfounded, as I was not sure of what was happening for a few seconds. Then my mind was reconnected. That was when I ran to the nearby street phone and dialed 911. The rests was history.

The way I preserved myself and my children was by my brave and pronounced response that shattered the heinous attitude of the thugs when I asked why. In addition, the Almighty was on the job to decrease the possibilities of my children's and my own demise. It was indeed among the most dramatic and unprecedented experiences I have ever had in my life. This aftermath lived with me for several years, and I suffered psychological trauma as a result. This meant I was unconsciously running traffic lights, driving the wrong way on a street, crying aloud at times, and experiencing nightmares. I even considered taking revenge if I could only find them, because my self-preservation was threatened, and the likelihood of it happening again was high. I was in constant self-preservation mode.

My family had to cope with a madman for several months. All the major television and radio stations and newspapers broadcast this narrative throughout most of the states of America, and men and women of the cloth throughout the States called my family and me to pray for us. Many of those folks knew us, and many did not. It was a somber time for us, as I had to coexist with a symptom of a mental disorder for several months. In addition, my family suffered for the same period because of my condition. It could not be overlooked and disrupted our lives and routines. Life taught me that we should not take anyone at face value. Evil is manifested in a man's heart and not in his face. As you can see a man's face but not his heart. I also learned that Hades has three gates: anger, lust, and greed; hence, the accomplished gunmen came after me, but if God is for you, who can be against you? Genesis 50:20 (NKJV) declares, "As for you, you meant evil against me, but God meant it for good, to bring it about as it is this day to save many people's lives." I finally learned that the Supreme Being could protect us from all evil. David declares in Psalm 23:4 (NKJV), "Yea though I walk through the valley of the shadow of death I will fear no evil for thou are with me; Your rod and Your staff, they comfort me.

Many years after this experience, I realized that you are only as good as your best self. Self-preservation is that cocoon that motivates you and brings to the fore, your best self. Scientifically speaking, caterpillars emerge from their cocoons as beautiful butterflies; prior to becoming a beautiful butterfly, it was an ugly caterpillar protected from the elements in a cocoon for a period before being transformed. The cocoon was the caterpillar's armor, which literally protected it from all harm and danger. Spiritually speaking, our armor as Christians is the Holy Ghost, who provides covering for us in our darkest hours.

Self-preservation techniques are necessary to accomplish any present and future task that you engage in. A *technique* is defined as a skillful or efficient way of doing or achieving something. Self-preservation techniques in a relationship should not be used in isolation but rather in observation and communication with your partner or spouse as he or she soon enough will have an increasingly crucial role in your self-remaining protected and thus your relationship. You are establishing a realistic scenario to prepare and make ready for your partner, just in the event anything out of the ordinary comes to pass when least expected. Life is certainly unpredictable, and you can never be overprepared, but you can be underprepared. More than 80 percent of preservation techniques have to do with strategic planning, listening, and preparation. The remaining 20 percent has to do with acting accordingly in a real situation.

If you have ever flown in a plane, you will remember prior to the plane taking off the attendant demonstrating to all the passengers all the techniques they should apply in the event the plane decides to go down or become involved in any accident or mishap. It is self-preservation that is always demonstrated when using the personal protective equipment (PPE). That is why they do a public demonstration with the PPE prior to the plane taking off. The importance of self-preservation cannot be clearer. It is expressed in so many ways in a public place, and the writing is on your heart. Just practice it.

How about self-preservation tools? An architect cannot design a building unless he has the right tools, nor can a builder build a structure unless he has the proper tools. Tools are necessary to produce professional work and are defined as devices or instruments, especially those held in the hand, used to carry out a particular function. There are circumstances when we are willing and ready to sacrifice our rights to live for something grander.

Since we are directed by our thoughts, to think, plan, and execute, we are forced to consider the brevity of our lives. As you can see, I am suggesting the self-preservation tools are our thoughts, our plans, and our executions. Permit me to put those three tools into perspective as it relates to self-preservation.

1. Thoughts are ideas or opinions that are captured by the mind. There are good thoughts and evil thoughts that follow you, depending on your ideologies, moods, or desires or even the circumstances you may find yourself in. You are the owner of your thoughts and actions, and ultimately, you are responsible for whatever transpires in the world of your thoughts.

Thoughts evolve into powerful constructs or objects when imagined. It is your imaginary insights that create lively and living realities. Psalm 33:9 (NKJV) exemplifies this: "He spoke, and it was done, He commanded, and it stood fast." Hebrew 11:3 (NKJV) says, "By faith we understand that the world was formed by the word of God, so that the things which are seen were not made of things which are visible." God spoke everything into being, and so you can see how your thoughts are a tool for self-preservation. Your thoughts send signals to your mind, and your mind tells you what to do. Your mind is liken to a battle field where good and evil encounter.

Someone said that the mind is a terrible thing to waste. Your mind is the tool that sustains your self-preservation. Your thoughts, coupled with your mind, are the initial tools used to get the work started and finished. Your mind and thoughts also answer the questions: how to do it, why to do it, and when to do it. This is what puts your entire body into motion and mobilizes you to do the best that you can do. This is awesome and powerful. How many times for a given moment where you compelled to do something you did not want to or plan to do? After you followed your inner being, you were happy. What propelled you? It was your thought that sent a signal to your mind, and the rest became history. The reason people function the way they do is because of their thoughts and minds working together for a common good, or conversely, they are not in sync. All your actions and reactions are scripts presented to you to perform good or evil. Evil scripts are infused into the system by the evil one.

Using your thoughts as a tool to be successful in the act of self-preservation at the highest level is possible. It will demand that very early in the process, you change your thoughts from bad to good. If you can only be disciplined enough to control and change your thoughts, you will automatically change your world, your reality, and even your perceptions. There is a true saying that if only you can control a person's mind, you can control his or her life. The only difference between a good day and a bad day is your attitude. How you receive the day matters.

2. Plan. This is an intention or decision of what you are going to do. Self-preservation demands strategic planning of all causes, as you are planning for any sudden eventualities. Anything can happen to anyone at any time, without any prior notice. Everyone is vulnerable where mishap is concerned, so preparation and planning are keys to combatting being hurt or injured blindly. I have mentioned the demonstration that the flight attendants showcase in the plane prior to takeoff. In essence, they prepare their passengers for self-preservation just in the event there is an accident or crash while in the air. However, planning is impacted based upon your daily activities.

For example, the foregoing scenario tells you of the attendants' daily activities. A flight attendant is one who is employed to look after the passengers on the aircraft. If someone is a sailor, working on a ship, his or her planning would obviously be different than the person who works on an aircraft. The only thing that remains constant is the planning, but the activities differ, and the method of planning will be different, as will the PPE equipment.

Let us talk about the activities and zero in on relationship-related activities, as they are the focus where self-preservation and utilizing the right tools are concerned. One must make plans to mitigate all unforeseen accidents or mishaps. The daily activity in this scenario is winning someone's heart and maintaining the attachment forever through intimacy, because the PPE will depend on where you are at the time of a mishap. For the most part, your main tool will be your thoughts and mind, but what would make it difficult is the fact that both partners must operate independently in the event of an accident while you are together. This would have to be communicated during planning.

Let's bear in mind that a plan or planning has to do with a detailed proposal for doing or achieving something while leaving room for errors and miscalculations but all the while trying to capture multiple scenarios and outcomes. In this scenario, the goal is to achieve maximum loyalty and commitment for each other. It is like inserting an oath into a deep-seated conversation, a conversation like no other because it has to do with life and death. It speaks value and demands both partners' honesty, especially at the appointed time of a sudden misfortune. Planning of this magnitude should never be taken for granted. Often, incidents can be avoided, but because of one or both partners' negligence, both partners end up suffering.

Planning will protect you from inflicting harm and self-destruction, and this will be essential to both of you to achieve success in your endeavors. In the process of preparing and planning, be mindful to build and execute a personal self-preservation plan that would aid you in combating anything that comes against either of you in your quest to achieve and express your intentions. There are two factors that could be part of your planning and implementation, and they are revaluating and reassessing the sharpness of your thoughts since thought changes in your life are inevitable, to an extent.

If, after evaluating and assessing the sharpness of your thoughts and mind, your findings are unacceptable, recognizing and seeking help is commendable. It is time for you to reach out for your lifeline. If your lifeline is proactively engaged in your preparation, your lifeline can alter escalation of sudden situations and prevent the need for emergency resuscitations. Your lifeline comes in diverse shapes and forms, from relaxation activities, such as walking or playing indoor games, to a spiritual mentor, such as a pastor or an elder whom you can trust to open up to and be honest with. This, of course, will rejuvenate your body and invigorate your emotional health.

Remember that life is filled with hindrances and traps that have their own objectives, most of which are to derail our motivations and successes. You do not want to get caught up with challenges that would literally wear you down and burn you out. I have been there several times in my life; it was not very easy getting consumed with work, family, chores, church activities, and events. That can happen to anyone who does not take time off periodically. You will find yourself mentally drained, physically tired, and emotionally frazzled. Subsequently, you will hit rock bottom before you know it, and there will be no quick fix for revival. It is often said that prevention is better than cure. I strongly recommend you find your lifeline and ensure you have a direct connection to it or him or her. Your lifelines can be objects, activities, or people.

You should not wait until there is a crisis in your life to come up with a crisis plan or a plan of action. You should plan enough or preplan to avoid finding trouble knocking at your door that you are unprepared for. One of the best approaches to planning in the context of self- preservation is to put together an action list of tasks that are relevant to the achievement of your goals and aspirations. Also plan for events that will naturally occur that oppose your goals. Decide how you plan to get back on course. Pen a good outline that will lead to *great outcome*. It will only help you to organize and stay focused on the tasks at hand. It may feel too far away today, but tomorrow it may seem even closer with some preparation. Jump into the driver's seat, and do not let life do the driving for you. Take control and stay on course. A plan helps you chart the direction of your destination.

3. The final tool that will chart your course for self-control is execution. Execution in the context of self-preservation is to put into effect a preparation and plan that was completed. Execution is the final call of mobilization after intensive, detailed, and thorough planning. The process of planning is completed when the green light of execution is turned on. This tool is only being used occasionally, and it is usually whenever there is an accident or mishap in our activities. Depending on the activities and the nature of the misfortune, execution can pose a danger for anyone who believes in and practices self-preservation in its purest sense.

One of the most despicable experiences that I suggest everyone may want to consider avoiding is using the execution to save yourself and then save someone else who is very close to you, without it being carefully thought through. It is a nightmare, especially if you have never gone through the process of thinking, planning, or executing. How do I know? Glad you asked. I have experienced the lack of ability to execute what could have been a deadly move. I talked about the almost deadly event in the previous chapter, when my two babies and I were attacked and shot at. Thanks be to God that even though my son got shot at six months old, we are all alive and are fine and healthy. Just writing about it brings back anger. I would not like anyone to have that experience or anything similar.

Safety should be first or given priority in all our activities. Regardless of whether our activities are indoors or outdoors, we should give priority to safety. For instance, the acronym OSHA stands for Occupational Safety and Health Administration; it was enacted in 1970 by Congress to ensure safe and healthy working conditions for working men and women by setting and enforcing standards and by providing training, outreach, education, and assistance.

Safety helps you to be aware of your surroundings or environment. On an average day, do you know the people who are around you or what is in your space? After you answer those two profound questions honestly, the next question will be do those things or people in your space raise any concern or pose any form of direct or indirect danger? If your answer is yes, then you must be prepared to execute your plan in accordance with whatever is available, within your reach, in response to these eventualities. Alternatively, if your answer is no, consider yourself blessed. For no one ever knows how an execution will turn out. So, plan your execution in a timely manner and execute your plan appropriately to receive the best value and the satisfaction that is intended.

You should consider both when and how to execute your plan, for the when and the how complement each other. If your execution is not done in a timely manner, it can ultimately become fatal both to you and your partner and ultimately your surroundings. Also, who and what occupy the space in question at the same time? Timing is everything, but it also waits on no one. You need to be time-conscious where execution is concerned. I have seen time and time again folks lose their blessings because they did not show up at the appropriate time to receive what rightfully belonged to them.

The main player in self-preservation is personal character. The way in which you navigate yourself during a crisis or unforeseen circumstances matters to you and the potential survivors around you. The results of a genuine mishap depend heavily on the characters involved. If the individual, at the end of the disaster, is proven to be of upward moral standing in the eyes of the public and is quick to anticipate and execute a countermove to the mishap, most likely, he or she will be handling the process in a professional manner, as opposed to the individual who is in the middle of the crisis and handling it poorly, which can lead to much disdain being directed toward that person. This person will more than likely be the one who will handle the process in an unprofessional manner. May I say that character plays an extraordinary role in self-preservation, and crises are known to reveal true character? Let us look at three ways you can maintain your character as it connects with self-preservation.

1. Do not conform to anything that is outside of your character in your attitude, the things you say or do, your belief system, your dress code, and the list goes on. The word *conform* means to give approval to something or someone, overruling your own convictions. Romans 12:2 (NKJV) declares, "And do not conform to this world, but be transformed by the renewing of your mind, that you may prove what is that good and acceptable and perfect will of God." You should not conform at any cost to false truths and fables, which have the potential to damage your character forever, should you be found to be associated. You should stand up for your own convictions even if you must stand alone—especially then. In extension, do not be afraid to stand alone. The scripture in this context declares that you should not conform but rather transform, meaning, you should embrace the fact that you will be different from the people in the world (the worldly people), that you will live differently, and this should be a distinction as it is noted in my previous comment regarding self-preservation. Your thoughts, your plans, your execution should be carried out in a professional manner. This speaks volumes because of the deliberate and humble approach by which you conduct yourself.

The final part of Romans 12:2 (NKJV) suggested "renewing your minds or allowing your minds to be renewed. Only then you may prove, acknowledge what is that good and acceptable and perfect will of God."

Your mind is like a computer or drive; it stores program files and all data files. The mind stores everything to enter and filters what is not needed. But the mind does not stand by itself. It is not independent. It works together with the thoughts. The thoughts send signals to the mind, giving it power to execute the decisions. Ultimately, our mind knows what God's will is for our life. Humanly speaking, if we only follow our inner spirit, we will also know God's will for our lives.

This is important because self-preservation does not function in isolation. It is not independent. It must coexist with humanity and their thoughts, plans, and executions. The driving force behind our thoughts from a spiritual perspective is the inner spirit that manifests through the Holy Ghost. Because man was not evolved but was created by God, man was created and made simultaneously. As human beings, we are made of three vital elements, which are spirit, soul, and body. John 16:13 (NKJV) declares, "However, when He, the Spirit of truth, has come, He will guide you into all truth, for He will not speak of His own authority, but whatever He hears He will speak, and He will tell you things to come." Billy Graham declares "the Holy Spirit illuminates the minds of people, makes us yearn for God, and takes spiritual truth and makes it understandable to us."

Make no mistake about the spirit inborn in every human. It gives us the ability to know right from wrong and good from bad. This statement qualifies my previous comment when I explained the contrast of an individual who has a high moral standing as opposed to another whose moral standing is poor and questionable, in essence, one whose morals need more work. The differences are being displayed whenever there is a crisis and a plan needs to be executed. The one that was transformed and not conformed by the worldly lifestyle will demonstrate a higher level of discipline and aptitude, at all costs.

2. Acknowledge and value the process of lessons learned. Lessons are learned when someone summarizes the positive and negative outcomes of a series of experiences regarding how they managed a particular project or situation. The difficult part of a lesson

learned is when you must analyze what exactly transpired during the project or situation and conclude either the positive or negative lessons learned. Acknowledgment is the most difficult task for anyone, especially if you were forewarned regarding the difficulty of the project or situation and you ignored the advice. In contrast, if the results turned out to be positive and fulfilling, acknowledgment would be forthcoming much faster with an attitude of gratitude.

For example, my wife and I got caught up in the business of renting a house for additional income to offset some of our expenses in the past. Even though we were told being a landlord in New York City was not an easy task, we gave it a few tries. Our first tenant was a public-school teacher and single parent with one daughter. She lived there for more than five years, and we never had a problem with rent or repairs. She was very quiet and cordial, easy to talk with and deal with. The day of her departure, she hired a carpet company to steam-clean and vacuum the carpet in all the rooms. She left the apartment in immaculate condition. I will never forget our first tenant for her honesty. Not long after she left, another tenant came to rent the house, but the lease was short-lived. This tenant paid one month's rent and one month's security deposit and then refused to pay the second one. We spent time and money going to court, trying to get this tenant out. Our court visits lasted more than four months before we were finally able to get rid of the tenant. Talk about frustration. Tenant number three lasted for three plus years, but we had to take this one to court for rent just like the previous one. Apart from her withholding rent, her children were also not well behaved. Subsequently and for our peace of mind, we got rid of these situations altogether.

Unfortunately, every other tenant was a disaster. They came in with one month's rent and one month's security, and the rest was history. We ended up in court for several months prior to tenants' vacating. The last tenant was so vicious, evil, and warlike, it was the final straw. It took my wife and me three and a half years to win, to get that tenant out of the apartment. The time and money required to take us back and forth to court was not easy, but it was worth it. One week prior to them vacating the apartment, we received a lawsuit letter from the attorney alleging a slip and fall down the stairs that caused injuries to our tenant's spine, and thus, she began walking with a cane outdoors—but indoors, she used no cane. Even though we swiftly undertook due diligence by engaging attorneys, the court would gladly award them $365,000 from our homeowner's insurance. Our compiled photo evidence and eyewitnesses did not matter to the courts and their attorney. Immediately after they vacated the apartment, we decided to stop renting the apartment and permit our children to occupy the place. There were a lot of lessons learned from those ten years of horror, lies, and evil from those tenants who passed through our apartment.

The first lesson learned was a lesson of regret because there were more losses than gains within the ten years, and we regretted the kind of family we rented the apartment to and the way they managed it. The characters of most of the tenants were toxic. They did not appear to be toxic prior to occupying the apartment, but after entry, everything else was chaos.

The second lesson learned as it relates to approving tenants is never to accept anyone's approval before you do your own vetting and assessment on the tenant in question. It is said that prevention is better than cure.

The third lesson learned was never to rent your house to Section 8 clients. They would forever find fault in your apartment because they know that the government will be on their side, giving them 100 percent support. Even when nothing was happening in the house, these tenants would report that something was wrong. For example, many days the heat would be way up, and they would call the city complaining that they had no heat, when in fact it was far beyond the required temperature.

The fourth lesson learned was to avoid renting your apartment to a large family. Preferably, rent to a couple with one child. Many children in your home will ruin your apartment. They will scratch the walls with pencils, pens, or crayons, and they will permanently damage your carpet with all kinds of liquids and dirt. We were reluctant to remove our carpet from the apartment. After the last tenant left, we had to remove all the carpet and convert it to a hardwood floor. This, of course, incurred additional expenses for us.

The fifth and last lesson learned was to follow your intuition. I was guilty of not charting the course of my instinct, resulting in making all the bad and terrible decisions. Our intuition is like a GPS, guiding us to our destination. You should not allow anyone to sway you in the opposite direction from your intuition. Instead, be led by your inner spirit. Intuition is your invisible compass. In the case of my wife and me, our time, money, energy, and strength were not worth it. We both learned from our mistakes, but if only we had listened sometimes to the right voices, we could have prevented it. It will do us good, especially with our health and finances. Lessons learned means lessons should be remembered. Forget what hurt you in the past, but never forget what it taught you. Remember, the most valuable lessons are not taught; they are experienced.

   3. Be yourself in public and in private. Self-preservation should not be done in a vacuum, separate or hidden, but rather in the public eye. A person who does not have moral standing on value will have the tendency to be hiding in public. If only integrity is being practiced, soon enough, it will become perfect. I have said repeatedly that integrity is what we do when no one is watching. There are many Christians who behave well in church—they speak well, ask great questions, and display good attributes—but privately, they are quite the opposite. The way they speak to one another, and their attitude being displayed are totally the opposite and, in some cases, utterly atrocious. They display no moral compass when they are in private but pretend in public because many people are there to see them.

Colossians 3:22 (NKJV) declares, "Bond servant, obey in all things your masters according to the flesh, not eyeservice as men pleasers but in sincerity of heart fearing God." The latter part of the scripture tells us that we should not be men pleasers but fear God in whatever we do and that it should be done unto the Lord and not unto men. This suggests that if your intentions are to please God, you should do it with excellent and high moral value.

It cannot be emphasized enough that character cannot be developed in isolation but by connection and community. It cannot be developed in ease and quiet. Only through trials and suffering can a moral person realize his or her potential. The test of authentic character is not defined by one's notoriety but by fortitude, both mental and physical, as they are made to endure for several years. Everyone has an ambitious projection to become famous, but hardly anyone is prepared to go through the process of bravery, pain, and adversity that is required, at least if that fame is to last. Life is filled with shortcuts, but you must go down the longest road to develop character that lasts.

Be careful with the mask you put on occasionally, as you might get used to it. A strong inner core foundation can be established by how a person builds character, especially when self-worth is a primary factor in shaping and molding the values and virtues of a balanced individual. With the absence of a strong core, self-developed with healthy self-esteem, personal goals and spiritual goals are directly impacted thus leaving one feeling confused about one's life circumstances. The conclusive and successful destiny of one's self-preservation hinges on the audacity of one's character.

15. UNDERSTANDING A RELATIONSHIP'S PROTOCOL

A relationship protocol is a code of ethics that prescribes strict adherence to correct etiquette and precedents related to the relationship. The relationship protocol guides both partners on ethical conduct and behavior prior to the manifestation of the relationship. The protocol is a relationship's road map throughout its journey, the guiding hand to move it from stage to stage. Unless a builder uses a formal and professional blueprint (drawing) to construct his or her product, he or she will not be doing justice to the project. What matters on that blueprint are the specifications and the scope of work required for that project to achieve desired results. The specification is the document from which the building is to be constructed, altered, demolished, or removed; in addition, the specification details the materials and products to be used, specifying every product names and the manufacturer's identification numbers or references. The scope of work is a detailed breakdown of all the line items pertaining to the intended project, from start to finish. Should the builder alter the specification or the scope of work in any form, shape, or fashion, it will influence the structure, and depending on the alteration, it could have a detrimental effect. Occurrences such as these will ultimately impede the structure, simply because the builder ignored protocols, for example, the building code or the code of ethics and best practices in the construction industry.

The code of ethics in a relationship protocol would yield the same results if the people involved practice it, without neglecting or negatively tampering with it. Every organization, institution, and informal relationship needs to establish a code of ethics to mitigate the rise of human animosity and prevailing insane behavior. I can ascertain that most, if not all, organizations and institutions have established codes of ethics that govern their employees' expected behavior. However, I have never heard of a code of ethics that has been established in our society for relationships; hence I am strongly convicted this is the reason there are so many pitfalls in marriages and relationships in general, and if left unchecked, there will continue to be these pitfalls for many future generations. The good news is there is hope, but hope can only transform futures if someone deliberately steps forward and implements it.

We must set up guardrails to protect the innocence of our society. One marriage ending in divorce is one too many, and consistently, statistics have been telling us that divorce is on the rise daily, especially at the beginning of this unprecedented COVID-19 pandemic. Here are five ethical precepts I am hereby documenting in this material for the first time with the hope that they will be looked upon as policies in the realm of a relationship protocol. Think of them as basic human rights, surrounding coexisting and relationships.

1. Responsibility and accountability
2. Devotion
3. Integrity
4. Respect
5. Honesty

1. RESPONSIBILITY AND ACCOUNTABILITY

Responsibility in this regard is an ethical concept that refers to the fact that partners in a relationship have shared responsibility and accountability toward each other. They also have morally based obligations and duties to adhere to outside of the relationship to make it work. Responsibilities refers to a set of assigned duties given for both partners to comply with. If there is no compliance, there will be no responsibility to adhere to, effectively ruining the entire concept of the code of ethics.

The role for each partner should be the same. They should take on their responsibilities and accountability to fulfill the role under an invisible oath of their conscience and promises to each other. While in this relationship, they will have an agreement of shared responsibility. Each partner's responsibilities should be more than just the basic function of the act of being in a relationship. Rather they should insert the multiple facts inherent to that role or function, which include both processes and outcomes. A responsible leader should be one whose job involves a predetermined set of rules and obligations that need to be met for him or her to be an effective leader.

According to Aristotle, a Greek philosopher, moral responsibility originated with the normal concept of decision-making and grew out of an ability to reason, an awareness of action and consequences, and a willingness to act free from external compulsion. Aristotle is not only addressing responsibility by normal means, which speaks volumes, but as morality, defined as principles concerning the distinction between right and wrong or good or bad behavior played out in a relationship.

Accountability is the readiness or preparedness to give an explanation or justification to both partners for one's judgments, intentions, and actions. Responsibility is defined as a rare obligation associated with a role. Accountability could be defined as blaming or crediting either partner or both partners for the actions. Accountability is a readiness to have one partner's actions judged by another partner, where appropriate.

Accept responsibility for errors, misjudgments, negligence, and recognition for competent conscientiousness, excellence, and wisdom.

Accountability can be difficult in the end if either partner is irresponsible in any way for his or her actions. He or she must accept some degree of accountability. Contrariwise, if responsibility and accountability are not equitably shared and if the process by which they are assigned is not stringent, then problems will inevitably arise. Abraham Lincoln once quoted, "You cannot escape the responsibility of tomorrow by evading it tomorrow." Responsibility and accountability are the magnet and steel in every successful relationship. If either is absent, the relationship will be one of inferiority in nature and character.

There are eight simple projected questions that will determine the level of your code of ethics being understood and executed in a timely manner.

1. Are you willing to share your partner's vision with any of your acquaintances?
2. Would you date another person because of a common misunderstanding between you and your current partners or spouse?
3. Are you constantly looking for opportunities to demean your partner on any level?
4. Is your conversation seasoned with salt or with bitterness when communicating in public?
5. What is your tolerance level when pushed by your partner?
6. Do you sometimes sense that the level of your responsibilities should be questioned?
7. About your accountability, do you take the blame for your own actions or negligence because of your poor judgment regarding your health?
8. Do you refuse to listen to your partner, resulting in a fight that causes mistrust in your relationship?

The right thing to do, if there is a heated argument between you and your spouse, is to try to deescalate or extinguish the fuse, but instead, you cause it to be escalated to a high degree.

You refused to recognize the seriousness of your relationship from the very beginning and now have no intention to think differently.

If the foregoing questions or concepts pertain to you, you are not yet ready for a commitment of this nature and magnitude. You are literally lacking judgment and the true substance that embodies the code of ethics in a relationship protocol. Permit me to quote James 1:5 (NKJV): "If any of you lacks wisdom, let him ask of God, who gives to all liberally and without reproach, and it will be given to him." Any requests for knowledge are a stepping-stone to finding the truth of all knowledge. He promised that you will not be reproached, upbraided, chastised, or put down. The promise here is that you will receive the knowledge that you request. Whenever poor judgment is being sewn into a heated argument, you will reap poor results.

You need to choose your battles wisely. Not every battle was meant for you, and the same strategy doesn't work for all battles. Some battles surface to build your tolerance level, and you must exercise patience at all costs. Circumstances come into your life to build your morals and to advance your strength and courage in times of severe adversity. You should, however, avoid hurting one another in thoughts, words, or deeds. The reality is that people do not hurt those they love intentionally. Only a fool or someone who didn't really love in the first place would do that. Rather, love will propel you to nurture, protect, and care for those things and people you love instead of beating and battering them.

There are too many partners and couples being abused, mentally, physically, emotionally, psychologically, and even sexually. Hence the reason for the code of ethics in the relationship protocol, which I believe should be mandated from an institutional viewpoint, as stated previously. From a church organizational viewpoint, this could be easily inducted into such an organization because state and church are two separate entities. The state is political, and the church is religious. They are self-governing in nature or independent of one another. They have the capacity to make an informed, uncoerced decision. In contrast, it would or cannot be adaptable through states' institutions because of the three branches of government, First Amendment rights, and red tape.

2. DEVOTION

Devotion is defined as loyalty to a person or cause. Studies have taught us that one of the causes of an unstable relationship is lack of fidelity or devotion. In contrast, relationships thrive much more when each partner has decided to be committed to the other by any cause. So, the antidote needed is to infuse strict adherence to following and maintaining the relationship protocol as a preestablished code of ethics for both partners. Exhibit 1 should highlight some of the dangers if either partner should violate these agreed-upon rules. People generally function much better when rules of strict adherence are implemented.

Often, people become neglectful of their initial goals and good intentions to do what they promised to do. The reality is that you are functioning in the violation zone when you are no longer dedicated to your spouse or partner, all the while expecting your partner to remain wholeheartedly devoted to you and the relationship. Dedication or devotion protocol is not a part-time job you have with your partner. It is a full-time job and investment that you signed up for. Being on standby or on call is not the same as protocol, it will not reap the same results. If you are not signing up fully from the beginning, you should not sign up, since there is no escape as it relates to the code of ethics in a relationship protocol.

Pilots are great examples of being devoted. After takeoff, they remain in their station until the plane lands and even after all passengers have disembarked unless there is an urgent call for them to be away, such as to use the bathroom. They are there to protect the well-being of the people and to ensure they have a safe flight to their destination. The same dedication or devotion is required for spouses and partners in a relationship. You should always be available for each other.

Unless you are suffering from attention deficit hyperactivity disorder (ADHD), which is a brain disorder marked by an ongoing pattern of inattention and or hyperactivity and impulsivity that interferes with functioning or development, devotion is not an unreachable stretch. If this is what is currently happening with you, it is just unfortunate. If it is not happening with you, your excuses are baseless, and you should be held accountable for the expectations you agreed to. The broad objective of the code of ethics to be introduced into relationship protocol is to promote unity for partners and spouses, but before unity can be accomplished in any relationship, accountability must be dealt with in the framework of your relationship.

Often, the one who has the advantage in the relationship wants to move on quickly after a bitter misunderstanding between the two of them. But history has repeatedly proved that reconciliation is required for a new beginning without any bumps in the continuous process. Make no mistakes about it, some relationships are intense and hard work, especially when one or both partners do not care to fully adhere to simple and general protocols. Rules were meant to be followed not to be rebellious with in making your own choices. Your choices need to be coordinated with your spouse's or partner's.

Every potential partner or married person wants to be a great wife or husband, and being devoted is one of the keys to achieving this. If partners are willing to make sacrifices for the sake of their marriages, their marriages tend to last much longer. Research has proven that devoted spouses are far more satisfied with their marriages and are less likely to be intimidated by outside intruders or even feel trapped or uncomfortable in the relationship. Devotion protocol is when you take every possible step to ensure that the one you care for is being taken care of, to the highest level.

The Bible gave us several examples of devotion in relationships. Here are a few. Ephesians 5:22 (NKJV) declares, "Wives submit to your own husbands as to the Lord," and Ephesians 5:25 (NKJV) says, "Husbands, love your wives just as Christ also loved the church and gave himself for her." The context of those two texts speaks volumes of the importance of devotion in the relationship. Both parties have an equal role to play in enhancing devotion in the relationship. Wives are demanding love from their husbands in every regard, while the husband is demanding submission from his wife. If both requests are honored, then it is safe to say both the code of ethics and relationship protocol would be successful and fulfilling.

In my own experiences, I have learned that to be a devoted husband is no easy task. It must be born in your DNA to maintain it. This does not mean that you will not be subject to mistakes periodically; instead, the difference is whenever you make an error, you are ready to own it and apologize with the same breath. If you cannot acknowledge when you are wrong, you will never be able to do the right thing. You will always be a brazen, argumentative person and subsequently turn out to be a pathological liar who is not good for anyone who is pursuing devotion by any means necessary.

Finally, I believe that devotion as an aspect of a relationship's protocol should be cultural or a lifestyle. We need to display the version in every area of our lives, in our speech, our attitude, the way we treat our fellow man, and what we say about people, especially those who have done us wrong. We are to evaluate ourselves and make personal recommendations that will affect changes in our character and moral standing. The height of our reverence should be seen, felt, and practiced. Only then can both spouses and partners conclude that they have met the criteria of true devotion.

3. INTEGRITY

Integrity means following your moral or ethical conviction by doing the right thing in all regards and circumstances, even when no one is watching you. The influence of fear causes many couples to do the opposite and act irrationally instead of rationally to please some people and satisfy their egos. The true test of integrity is manifested during pressure, and pressure is exerted sometimes to squeeze the wrong out of you and leave the truth on the inside of you. Not every person likes to get rid of the wrong, and loosening the transitions that cause lots of problems is not an option for them.

Integrity in the relationship protocol should not be ignored. I am afraid if you ignore integrity, dishonesty will spread like wildfire. Abraham Lincoln once said, "Commitment is what transforms a promise into reality." Commitment is the ingredient character is made of. It has the power to change the face of things. It is the daily triumph of integrity over skepticism. In summarizing, Abraham Lincoln is saying integrity is not possible in the absence of commitment. They should be engraved in both partners' DNA and be manifested through their daily actions.

Please remember that the code of ethics is the engine of what charts the course of your actions in a professional manner. It highlights your honesty and integrity at all costs. Integrity is the glue between you and your spouse. It holds the partners together even when a strong wind of distraction and division is raging in the relationship. Make no mistake about it: ever so often, the winds of discouragement will blow fiercely to disband you from your commitment. You need to recognize your commitment was not for a moment but rather for longevity. Think about a sailor who gets caught with the boisterous wind in the middle of the ocean. Does he abandon his ship and jump overboard, or does he remain inside and fight until he overcomes it?

Likewise, you need to stay put and fight until dishonesty ceases and integrity is reborn. If your spouse has integrity, then you will feel secure about your marriage. You know if an unexpected crisis or disaster hits that you can count on him or her to act in an honorable way. Universally speaking, disaster has a way of bringing families, friends, spouses, and even enemies together. In the beginning of time, both good and evil existed, and both continue to prevail today.

Why does protocol matter in integrity? As I stated in my previous comment, integrity is the foundation on which every successful relationship is built. Bear in mind that there are some structural components that are necessary to construct that foundation. To be clearer, let us look at a steel bridge, which in fact is a steel structure. Any bridge without structural integrity will collapse, and there is no difference with human beings. The same principle applies. It is human beings who design and build those bridges. You would not want to drive on those bridges if you knew most of the engineers who designed and constructed them lacked moral standing or their moral values were next to nothing.

Of course, you would prefer to drive on a bridge that was built by an engineer whose character and moral compass were up to standard. This engineer is alert and focused on delivering quality bridges with no errors. He or she does this simply because he or she is a person of character, honesty, and value excellency. A great relationship needs to be designed and built with the same attitude and character that the engineer possesses.

4. RESPECT

Respect means that you show great recognition for your partner in spite of his or her shortcomings. Let him or her realize that he or she is a whole person to you and not just a way to get something that you want. Respect is the cornerstone of every healthy relationship. You show me a healthy couple, and I will tell you it is because they have their own integrity and respect. This shows a high level of regard because it means that you are aware that your partner has different experiences and opinions from you, and that is okay. Respect should flow from a pure heart and not be practiced loosely to satisfy one and dissatisfy the other.

A simple protocol needs to be established, followed, and maintained as it relates to respect in relationships. Rules were established to prevent accidents and possible death. This was the reason why traffic lights were invented. Protocol in arena of respect is to demonstrate love and care for the opposite sex.

Partners should demonstrate sincere and mutual love at all costs.

Readiness to accept a partner for who he or she is is the highest act of respect. If you have no intention to demonstrate respect to your fellow human, you should endeavor not to start a relationship.

When there is mutual respect and honesty in a healthy relationship, partners do not lie to each other or cover up truths.

In most relationships, women need love, but men prefer respect. Both partners should be transparent on public and private platforms.

Trust is essential in a relationship. It is more than believing that your partner would not cheat on you. Rather, you trust your partner with your actions. Actions always speak louder than words. It is not so much what you say to your spouse but what you do.

Are you reliable? Can you be taken at your word? Can you trust yourself? If you are not taking responsibility for your own actions, then you should not be trusted by your partner. How can you be trusted when you say you are going to the mall but end up at the movies without ever being at the mall? Are you always late? Are you constantly making plans and canceling at the last moment? Saying you will show up and not doing so is an act of unreliability and not being accountable and fair to your partner. You can reconcile this by setting time and date reminders on your calendar. Being dependable is showing respect for your partner's time and energy, which he or she put out to demonstrate respect for you. When you do the opposite, it causes chest pains and mistrust to creep into the bond that was established.

Let your words be seasoned with salt when communicating with each other. Communication is one of the most important parts of any relationship. The survival of any relationship solely depends on communication, even if both parties adopt sign language as a means of communication. Being open and honest with your partner means that you are open and honest with yourself. Often, you expect your partner to be a mind-reader, especially when you go on lockdown because you are not in agreement with your spouse. You need to speak up and never be afraid to speak your conscience. This way, your partner will not feel as though he or she is being ignored.

You should validate your spouse's or partner's feelings by acknowledging his or her pain or disagreement. Let him or her know that you heard what he or she is saying. Your partner needs to feel a part of you. Feeling uncomfortable will close the doors toward transparency and freedom to express him- or herself. To know your partner intimately, you need to spend time talking to him or her. You need to understand what is in the heart. Luke 6:45 (NKJV) says, "A good man out of the good treasure of his heart bringeth forth that which is good and an evil man out of the evil treasure of his heart bringeth forth that which is evil. From the abundance of his heart his mouth speaks."

Communication reveals one's intentions, character, and ideologies. You can use communication as a marker to determine your love-tank level. It can also be used to assess the level of one's commitment. Your partner's level of commitment can change, based upon moods, his or her level of satisfaction, feelings, and the way in which he or she is being treated. When it comes to conversation, women are much more talkative than men. Women use an average of twenty thousand words per day compared to the seven thousand men utter. Most women are far better communicators than men. Communication can make or break a relationship; both partners or spouses should consider establishing several ground rules to maintain stricter protocols. Here are eight ground rules that you need to consider.

1. Have good judgment of each other's behavior. Even though good judgment can be used as a marker to identify your partner's strengths and weaknesses, it can be one of the most damaging weapons in a relationship. It tells your partner that it is not okay to be him- or herself. This contributes to resentment and will eventually corrode even the most intimate relationships. Even if your relationship survives the corrosive effect of judgment, it still suffers. So, one must be careful not to use one's judgment skills to demean one's partner but rather to evaluate his or her

behavior and encourage him or her to do better. If both of you need to reconcile, just do it and move on in the name of peace with your relationship.

2. Authorize one speaker at a time. Always when communicating with your partner, you should avoid talking over each other. If your partner has the floor, as the intended receiver, you should listen attentively to reply accurately. Often, the receiver misunderstands because of poor listening skills, which can result in name calling, physical and psychological abuse, and sometimes divorce; yes, poor communication in the long term can lead to divorce. This can be avoided only if each partner follows the ground rules to wait his or her turn before speaking and speaks calmly instead of getting loud and excited, which would escalate things without any solutions. Sometimes it is not what we say but how we say it. You can incite anger by your tone. Learn to choose your battles and control yourself in the worst circumstances.

3. Be on the same page with the meaning of key words. Having the same mind or being like-minded is essential in relationships, especially when it comes to certain key words being used. This is commonplace, especially among couples and partners of different cultures. Nevertheless, you can agree to disagree or disagree to agree, but at the end of the day, both of you need to be seeing eye to eye.

4. Deal with the issues, not the person. Fundamentally, during a heated argument, most of you bombard your partner with harsh and unkind words. You abuse him or her mentally and stress him or her out, when, in fact, you should have gotten to the reason why the argument began by getting to the root of the issue. You are calling your spouse names because she missed her flight. The issue in question is that she was late getting to the airport because of an accident, which subsequently caused a traffic jam. It was not any fault of hers. So, talk about why she was late, and do not throw stones at her. This attitude will

mitigate stress on your part and remove the shadow of her being disrespectful to you. Lesson learned: ask questions before you assume things.

5. Keep the discussion on the subject matter. People communicate for several reasons, to name a few, sharing information, exchanging ideas, asking questions, and offering choices. Depending on the trend of your communication or your intent, you will have to stay on topic to accomplish your goal or purpose. Depending on how important the nature of the conversation is, multiple tasks should not be an option for either partner. You cannot be all over the place and create confusion in your partner's mind. If you are having a conversation about the most recent mob attack on Capitol Hill on January 6, 2021, and suddenly change to the snowstorm last night in New York City, your partner will get lost and will be totally confused in the process. Remember the biggest problem in communication is the illusion that it has taken place.

6. Bring your concerns to the table. Explore your concerns, pains, dissatisfaction, and dislikes, instead of sweeping them under the carpet, which will not help you in any way. The genesis for your healing is at the table with your partner where you can exercise transparency. Transparency is removing the mask and revealing truth in every situation or crisis. It is getting beyond the surface of what is really going on in your heart. Authenticity requires vulnerability, transparency, and integrity, and you're not better off not realizing your weaknesses, as you would then forget your strengths. Everything should be put on the table for discussion whenever there is a problem. The good, bad, and indifferent should have a place at the table. There are some relationships where one person is intimidated by his or her partner for diverse reasons. This should be a no-brainer, since it can weaken the relationship. Relationships should be constantly progressing and not regressing. My wife and I agreed very early

in our relationship to bring everything to the table. If need be, we still do it after thirty-three years.

7. Explain your side and your reasoning. Because you do not challenge the way you see things in a conversation, you do not develop the muscles that allow you to engage in productive conversation. Explaining the reason leading to your concluded conviction is the most important element of straight talk. Departing from it can cause communication to collapse in a moment. You will need to challenge your partner's comments and not just accept the assumptions he or she makes and then conclude the discussion.

8. Identify missing facts. It has been said a person is innocent until proven guilty. The markers being used to prove a person guilty are the evidence or facts being carefully vetted or evaluated. There is no difference with crooked conversations between partners, where the partners cannot understand one another because of the lack of critical information, which could be detrimental to the relationship. In such cases, the parties would have to validate the comments by producing necessary data, such as time, people, places, and photos to name a few types of evidence. This would allow the conversation to be credible and converted into straight talk. You need the appropriate data to substantiate truth in difficult and challenging conversations that are heading downhill.

These eight laid-out ground rules each work in conjunction with the others toward sharing, learning about, and understanding complex issues in relational communication.

5. HONESTY

Honesty is a facet of moral character that connotes positive and virtuous attributes, such as integrity, truthfulness, straightforwardness, and good conduct, along with the absence of lying, cheating, theft, and bias, to name a few. Honesty also involves being trustworthy, loyal, and sincere. Dishonesty is quite the opposite, especially where the question of religion is concerned. People are guilty of every possible sort of dishonesty and intellectual misdemeanor. Dishonesty, however, can be viewed as a learned behavior or even hereditary. If it is the foundation you learned, you can unlearn it. Whatever you learn, you have the ability and capacity to unlearn the same.

Honesty is a key component of all healthy and respectful relationships not only because it helps you to avoid harmful breaches of trust but because it allows you to live instead of fantasizing and to share this reality with someone special. Let us look at some tips as it relates to adequacy and precedence in relationship protocol.

First, always be ready to hear the truth, even though the truth may hurt. No one likes to hear the truth when he or she is in the wrong. For the good of the relationship, you should always prepare to hear the truth and be quick to acknowledge your wrongdoing and sincerely apologize to your lover. Remaining in denial only escalates a riot that you might regret and potentially, your relationship may not recover from. Remember that honesty is the best policy. If you practice being honest, you will be perfected after a period. Saying sorry will not make you any less of a person, but it will help your partner to trust you more, as honesty is another way to validate your partner.

Second, be honest with your rebuttal. Being on the wrong side of the fence or being caught with your pants down, you will want to challenge your accusations when being spoken to with your rebuttal. Remember when rebutting, you are at the mercy seat, not your partner. The noose is over your head ready for you to hang yourself. This is the moment you want to plead for pardon and not for the noose to be put over your head. Your reason for doing what you did should be honest, and you should display some degree of remorse for your actions. Try not to talk over your partner also. Be patient and polite.

Third, talk over things as they occur. You should never allow the sun to go down on your wrath. This means, prior to retiring to bed, you should settle any or all differences and misunderstandings that have occurred during the day. The older the issues, the hotter the battle will be. Resolve them immediately if possible, and go on to the next chapter in your life.

Fourth, avoid being judgmental. Encourage open and transparent dialogue. If you want to be more open with each other, both of you will have to stop being disparaging. When you feel judged, you will either become agitated or defensive or shut down. None of these options encourages open dialogue. Being humble and open to what the other has to say will let honesty be manifested over time.

CONCLUSION

Throughout this book, I have reinforced the importance of preparation. Every facet of one's life can have implications on how successful the relationship will be. This journey is best taken with both partners. Both partners should assess themselves as individuals and determine what they would like to make of the relationship. They must agree to support each other's introspection and growth.

If all else fails, please reach out to your Christian counselor or pastor as you navigate the world of relationships.

www.ingramcontent.com/pod-product-compliance
Lightning Source LLC
Chambersburg PA
CBHW030243010526
44107CB00030B/1321/J